Evan's

Torres Strait
CLOSE SHAVES & GEMS

Evan's CLOSE SHAVES & GEMS

Book 1
Torres Strait
Chronicles of the early 1970's

Close Shaves & Gems Series ~ Memoirs Of Evan

ISBN: 978-0-9581444-0-7

The publisher acknowledges and pays respect to the past, present and future traditional custodians and Elders of this nation and the continuation of cultural, spiritual and educational practices of Aboriginal and Torres Strait Islander peoples. Aboriginal and Torres Strait Islander peoples should be aware that this publication contains references to, or names of, people who have passed through transition.

A Leonbooks Publication

A catalogue record for this book is available from the National Library of Australia

for Charlie

Evan's
Torres Strait CLOSE SHAVES & GEMS

A brief glimpse into the bright dimension that is the Torres Strait and a compendium of adventures recounting high risk incidents that took place in a young man's life on land and sea at the Northern tip of Australia, the Torres Strait and the Coral Sea, this book is a tribute to the outstanding humanity of people in a unique realm of experience!

Big eso to my Islander family and friends.
My thanks to Leslie, Lorraine, Kim and all the others
who helped to make this book possible.

Prologue

Book 1 - Torres Strait CLOSE SHAVES & GEMS deals with things that happened in the early 1970's.

Not so long ago while driving quietly home a driver on substances suddenly crossed the median strip and drove straight into my car. With no time to evade, my vehicle was a write off. Sometime afterwards a good friend suggested that I put some of the close shaves that I had throughout my life on paper. It was true, this was yet another close shave as my friend reminded me.

Truth being stranger than fiction and looking back I can now see that perhaps many of the circumstances in this book were far more dangerous than at the time I may have imagined them to be. On the spot you don't have time to analyse much. You simply deal with the situation as best as you can. Reality is not like movies. You are there in multiple dimensions more than a flat screen. Consider that carefully.

The old cliche, "Expect the unexpected," holds true. It is a good way to navigate life! The other of course is, "Be prepared." If you are going to be travelling, doing it preparedly is to be preferred. Often in a high speed emergency there is no time to think or to behave irrationally. When travelling to different territories of experience it is always good to find out in advance and preferably have a reliable local guide. However as the emergency services can attest even in the suburbs there are no guarantees.

Survival is part of existence. Safety and security needs ongoing maintenance. Necessarily, the challenge principle is innate in the universe and at the core, raw Nature has one simple rule: Get it right or die!

Timing! What determines when you come and when you go? What impulse? Have you ever considered that leaving a few seconds earlier or later will change the whole dynamic of what follows and whether and how you are involved in an incident or miss it altogether?

At an interpersonal level social lubrications such as courtesy sometimes go a long way. At other times you need to deploy real skills, many which can be acquired through regular practice.

The 'Close Shaves' book series is not about the barber but rather barbaric situations and close shaves with the grim reaper at the hands of nature and its denizens simply doing their job in the life support system of the planet or dangerous people of bad intent who had lost their way as human beings.

Bullies are everywhere. Bullies are cowards. They live in fear and ignorance. People of decency and respect are everywhere too. Inaction in the face of injustice, that age old human pandemic of interpersonal violence, means adding to the suffering of those who have no voice such as victims of child abuse, domestic violence and other unnecessary and avoidable cruelty. With each act of disrespect there are consequences which in the end affect us all and contaminates humanity.

It need not be this way. Cruelty is always avoidable. Especially when sanity, empathy and respect prevails. Simple humanity. This of course begins at home. As for nature's high risk events they are more than enough to keep us psychologically fit exercising forward thinking, risk mitigation and driving those of us who have enough sense to care in making a healthier world.

Some people have commented in disbelief at some of the events portrayed here but the fact is that high risk work is performed daily by numerous people who don't write about it. It's all relative. I myself am in disbelief at a good friend who survived commuting and working in an office for 48 years!

Everyone experiences one or two high risk or near death events in a lifetime. Most either do not live to write about it or can't be bothered sharing the value of the lessons learned. As I get older my recollections have returned as vividly as a movie being replayed and so I finally gathered my notes and got this book down.

Things happened as they happened. Enjoy the journey!

Best Wishes, The Author

Contents

Contents

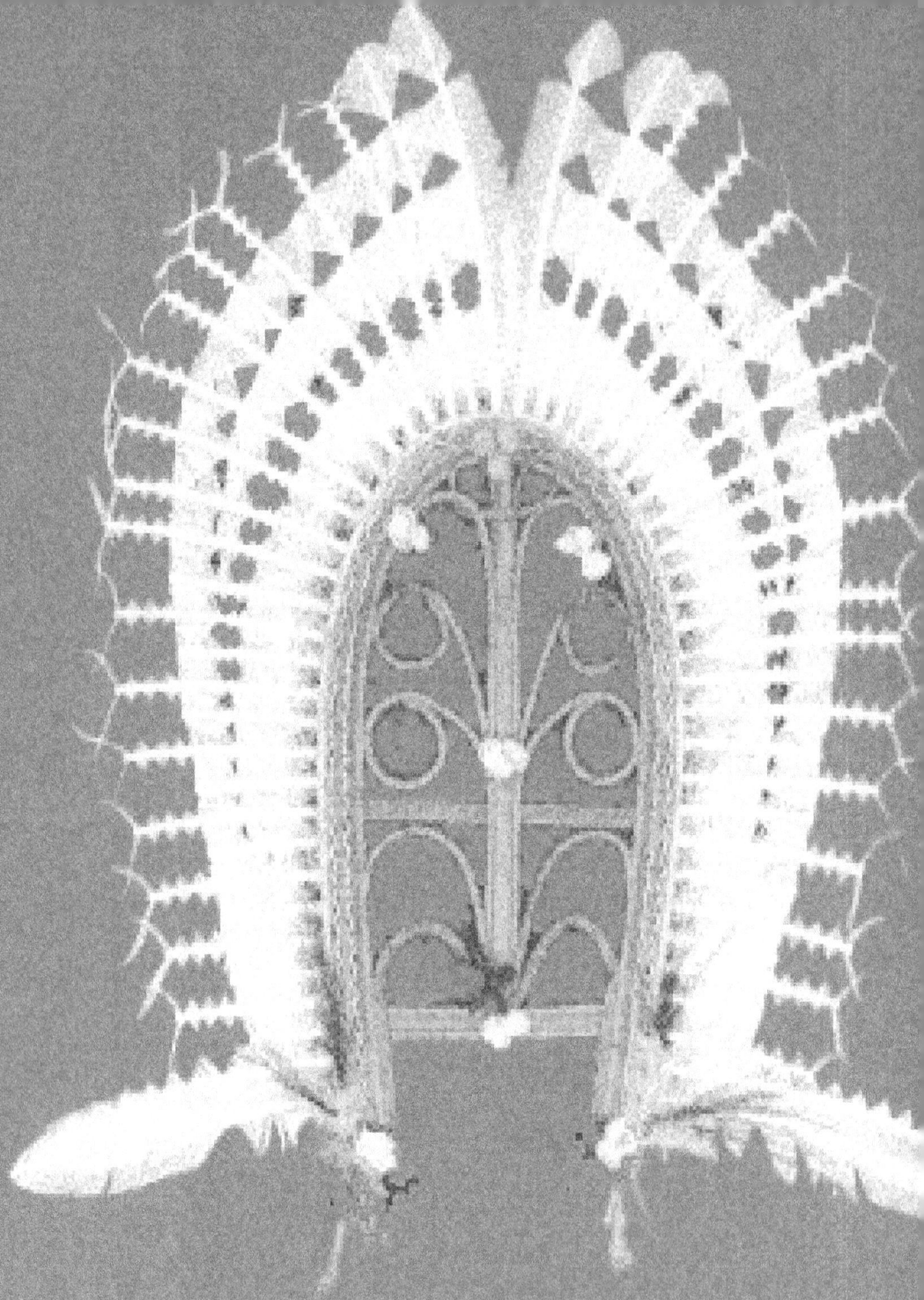

1. Erub - Learning The Way

Finally I got to see the island that I had heard so much about. The unbroken days at sea, a new and transformative experience, an entirely new dimension even more than Port Douglas had been. As a child I had read about such places but now I was here and it was real. So very real. The salty tang of oceanic breeze, the burning sun, the undulating waves augmented only by the forward motion of the motor vessel cutting through the waters swooshing uninterrupted by raucous city noises. Crystal clean primordial elements combined to strike a chord into the depths of my soul… undefinable dimensions.

A feeling of growing expectation took hold of me. Searching the horizon as if by instinct, unsure of what to expect, time passed. Suddenly there it was… a thin sliver, a shape I somehow recognised. The emotions I felt were indescribable as if I was coming alive for the very first time… slowly drawing nearer, the island gradually grew out of the ocean into its full magnificence. Tears welled up. It was a homecoming.

We anchored outside of Medigé Bay at Darnley Island and rowed ashore.

The Frenchman had been delivered into the hands of the local police and was now a guest of Her Majesty waiting to be taken to the courthouse at Thursday Island to be duly processed by the law. The MV 'Melbidir' was due in about three weeks and would convey him to his chosen fate. Melbidir was the Torres Strait supply boat which did the regular rounds of the islands.

There was feasting and joy at the return of Paul the Elder. The moment we first landed, Paul was called to a meeting of Elders and I was left to my own devices but I was not abandoned. It was not too long before I was accosted by a bevy of athletic beauties impressed by the light tan they didn't often see. All slender, lithe, well proportioned and fit, except one who was a large girl with rippling muscles and abs. Entirely feminine and lovely the young women introduced themselves surrounding me and asking me all manner of questions. The nearest ones wrapped their arms around mine and offered to escort me around the island for a guided tour. It was difficult to resist.

It was as if I had been transported to some other planet.

My stupid questions, "Where are the gyms?" and, "What do you do for protein supplements?" landed on uncomprehending ears and evinced giggles. It would take me a while to realise that the gym was lifestyle and the supplements were the vast array of natural uncontaminated foods. No artificiality here.

Together we traversed much of the island and they showed me the sights. The Island was a beautiful place.

To me it was mythical beyond anything I had ever hoped to experience in this life and the welcoming committee was delightful. I got back late.

Receiving numerous invitations to dine, for a few days we were obligated to accept them even though it would not be easy to keep them all, not so much because of time constraints as because of the amount of food we could eat. Tradition and good manners demanded it and the messengers were sent back and forth with thank-you's and confirmations. We spent a few days like this doing the rounds to visit kinfolk and relatives.

It had been a long time since Paul had been home and he would make the most of it. Relaxing, feasting and socialising while waiting for the right weather conditions.

Not long after, we set about preparing for work which would consist of towing several 12 to 14 foot dinghies behind the mother boat, the MV 'Ina' to selected locations and then going further out in the smaller vessels, usually in pairs, onto and around a reef to free dive and hand spear crayfish.

The tails would be snap-frozen and delivered to buyers at Thursday Island who would then distribute the cray (or lobster) as an exotic delicacy to restaurants around the world. Buyers would pay meagrely and we, the high-risk slaves got paid the equivalent of sweet fuck all. Which is not much. Pocket money.

But life at sea was good. I was young and loved it.

Out of magnanimity Paul allowed me to try out but lacking the experience of an Islander I was a typical clumsy 'white boy' who sat and looked at the fish, trying to aim the spear while the fish got bored with the game and swam away. I would return with an empty dinghy.

"Well that won't do," Paul said with a smile. I pleaded to try again. He agreed. I failed again and again.

Eventually he had to say with a stern tone in his voice, "I'm running a business here. You are not catching any fish. I can't have you wasting resources like this. It's woman's work for you. You can be the cook. Try not to stuff that up too.." It was teasing of course but it stung. It was probably intended to sting.

Whilst I was dismayed, he with the wisdom of Solomon put me through the ropes at a practical level starting with what I could do more safely.

Someone made the derogatory comment, "Emi sarupa," in translation, 'He's a drowned person, rejected by the ocean.' In my defence Paul replied, "Emi no sarupa, banbai we give him chance!"

In the beginning I was still a daydreamer and tended to drift into the thought world and… well I had stuffed up a batch at the sugar mill at Mossman… ruined several attempts at making damper at the cattle station and I had to concede, despite my youthful ego that he had a point!

For a few months I was boat cook mastering new skills through trial and error, the speed of learning probably augmented by a slight fear of a hungry crew of hard workers.

Once I learnt to prepare food well, I enjoyed it so much that I thrived on it. With daily practice I became a good sea-chef and my cuisine was respected.

Eventually I asked to be allowed to fish again. Our method was to dive in and grab or hand-spear the fish instead of waiting for them to bite. With cray there was no other way.

Paul kept his word. He gave me the chance that he had promised. I rigged up, took off in a borrowed dinghy and got into the water. I wanted to do more than cook.

Yet again in my first few attempts I tried and failed.

I could not return to the mother boat without at least something! Worried about being relegated to only menial tasks again I sat in the dinghy for a bit and contemplated how to get a result.

I craved to be in the water as well as the other tasks which I had mastered pretty well by now. What was I to do?

'Fuck it,' I thought, 'just do it!' With nothing left to lose I stopped trying so hard. Instead of stuffing around trying to aim I trusted my instincts then let loose without pause. The aiming would have to take care of itself, win, lose or draw! This is a great secret. It worked. To everybody's surprise I filled the dinghy and returned with lots of fish as well as lobster.

We stocked the refrigerator and ate better than ever. Everyone was pleased but none as much as I was.

Sometime later at Thursday Island I bought long flippers, a snorkel and a torn wetsuit from a young white man who was selling them before returning down south to the 'big smoke.' They were old but in good working order and for a nominal price I bought the lot. I ended up throwing away the wetsuit.

I finally saved enough to buy the right material to build myself a skiff, a fourteen footer. I would have loved a clinker but they were not so easy to acquire and I lacked the skill and resources to build one. I rejected an offer for a cheap aluminium one because they act like a sail. You cannot tow an aluminium dinghy whilst swimming, instead in the wind they can tow you into danger. So I built mine from raw timber and marine ply.

That was to be my small boat in the ocean for a few years. Every day before the sun came up, my little vessel would take me out into the Great Pacific Blue!

I never looked back. The fins were to give me an immense advantage. The Islanders nicknamed me 'Beizam' the shark, because I would swim around like a shark, never missed and always brought back a very good catch.

As incredulous and impressed as anyone else was at first, I soon took it for granted. I had passed the test.

Our mission was to gather crayfish which were prolific at the time and one of the last 'resources' which had not been fished out by intensive exploitation of the region.

Queensland salt water cray, whose proper title is, 'lobster' take from one to three seconds to capture once spotted and whilst averaging about a foot to a foot and a half in length (30 to 45 centimetres) can grow up to two feet or more in some instance. (60 centimetres) The big ones can weigh up to 4 kilos (about 8.5 pounds) although most averaged 2 to 3 kilos (4.5 to 6.5 pounds.) The smaller ones were not worth catching. The destiny of the ones we bagged was to grace the restaurants of the world.

It was a wasteful industry. Buyers only wanted the tails. Unskilled marketeers not understanding sustainability were in a hurry. Commerce being as it is, we were constrained to follow the party line or lose out and so we chucked the heads overboard squandering a resource which could have doubled profits.

As skill improved with daily practice, I would fill the dinghy nearly every time from the endless abundance that still existed in the ocean. Around fires and when chatting back in the islands, Paul would proudly boast how he had taught me. He would say, "I'm really proud of my son, he's next best after me." I never argued.

In some cultures this might have sounded strange but here it was a great honour to be next best in skill to an Elder, even if you caught a few more fish than him occasionally. Besides, I had an unfair advantage. Those flippers and that snorkel.

I was fortunate to be in this wonderful dimension.

From that day onwards the nickname 'Beizam' stuck. I thought nothing of it at the time. In order to return early to cook I would compete with myself to bring back a full catch in half the usual time and mostly succeeded. The crew were enjoying hearty meals every day and stopped mocking!

The challenge of successful time management and multi-tasking kept my mind busy, which is what I needed in those days.

No more 'sarupa' now Beizam, life was good!

2. Somerset Mangoes

We stopped briefly at a settlement now named Somerset.

Happy friendly people live there despite dispossession and deprivation that never existed before the invaders came. An unforgettable memory of the Northernmost Peninsula of the Australian land mass is that of fully natural rainbow coloured mangoes as large as a football with a better-than-ice cream flavour that is out of this world!

The indigenous communities here live in natural abundance in a huge region of unique biodiversity that forms one of the largest remaining unspoiled wilderness areas in the world.

The Cape York Peninsula is a large and remote area in the far north of Queensland. Its eastern coast borders the Coral Sea and is mostly rainforest. Its western coast the Gulf of Carpentaria contains thousands of species of native birdlife with large areas of proliferating eucalyptus woodland savannahs, stringy-bark, melaleuca, heathlands and wetlands.

The abundant variegation found here now finally recognised as having a major environmental importance for the planet but sadly not before a great portion was denuded for grazing cattle and sacred areas destroyed for mining. Introduced species and weeds are threatening the ancient homeostatic balance of both fauna and flora.

On the eastern side of the Peninsula Range there are many undisturbed rivers including the Lockhart River and the Endeavour River which flow to the Coral Sea and the Great Barrier Reef. These rivers are lined with thick rainforests, sand dunes and mangroves.

Aboriginal history on the Cape dates back tens of thousands of years when the land mass was conjoined with Papua in a natural land bridge possibly destroyed by the most recent cataclysmic megafauna extinction, the great global flooding of about 12,800 years before present time, a period known as The Younger Dryas where major geological disruption and changes abruptly took place. When the land mass subsided, the previous land bridge formed a great shoal shelf, an area of two thousand five hundred square kilometres or about a thousand square miles traditionally known as Lumudhal now known as Torres Strait or Zenadth Kes.

Following that event, the climate then took about 1,200 years to stabilise, slowly starting to emerge out of an ice age around 11,600 years ago and in the aftermath the long struggle of our most recent prehistory then restarted. The mass destruction of that event brought about colossal changes to land mass, environments, climate and of course people.

Notwithstanding, kinship relatives and connections continue across the divide to this very day. What remains of what once had been an at least 300 kilometre wide land bridge is now the Torres Strait Islands!

At the time of the more recent European invasion, the Cape York region consisted of forty-three tribal nations each with its own language and traditional practices. Although many of the languages have now been lost, an estimated ten languages and possibly hundreds of dialects continue to be spoken. Today Aboriginal communities are dotted all over the Peninsula with diverse histories, cultures and languages. Traditional civilisations are not as simplistic as they are often portrayed.

The area renamed, 'Cape York,' is now a cluster of 'developed' townships including Mapoon, Weipa and Bamaga and some other spots of great natural beauty.

Invasions have come and gone. The first European settlement was established at Somerset, Cape York in 1863.

The Earth is always there. We walk on the bones of our ancestors. The sun shines with equanimity on all. Those often violent invaders have now been consumed by the very land that they sought to steal and are now reduced to dust, forgotten in ignominy.

Some of the First People, custodians of that land still remain as do their traditions and customs.

My brief experience at this place was that these are happy people living close to the harmony of nature and doing their best against the odds of an often intense climate. The imposed deprivation caused some sadness but they still have the spiritual integrity to choose to be happy and optimistic.

They grow the best mangoes in the world!!

We stopped there for a while, ate mangoes and traded while Paul visited kinsfolk.

Not long after, we left on our mission of fishing, social bridge building and life!

3. The Best Fight I Did Not See

The best fight I didn't see happened on my first night at Thursday Island.

We arrived and dropped anchor in the bay outside. We had come from Darnley Island with a few stops on the way. Paul and some others had already been ashore on business and most stayed on land visiting relatives. I had remained on board and was still on the boat when Paul and one other returned.

By now it was night!

I recall looking out towards the land at Thursday Island and a foreboding feeling such as one might expect in a war zone hit me hard in the gut. Then Paul said, "We're going ashore again."

I did not want to go. We went!

It was myself, Paul and one of the other crew. We were going to walk to 'Tamwoy-Town' to visit Paul's relatives and let them know that we had arrived. The final visit for today. Uncle Yungup and family were going to billet us overnight before we left in the morning.

Clambering into a dinghy we rowed ashore. It was a dark moonless night and rowing would be safer than speeding by outboard motor. Besides, there was the risk of theft so we left the outboard on the mother boat.

On reaching the shore we secured the dinghy and set off on foot. We had walked a considerable distance around the island.

Just past the cemetery, without warning a speeding car screeched to a halt in front of us. The high beam blinded us and then it was switched off effectivity knocking out our night vision. At least for me. I could see nothing.

Hearing what sounded like angry men pouring out of the car it became obvious they were set upon attacking us. It was a ute full of Islanders on the warpath.

There was no time to think! Even I the daydreamer understood that this was trouble and that it was a bad moment. So with all my fantastic dojo training, judo, karate, aikido, weaponry and all that mighty stuff... I shaped up.

As I waited for the 'fight to start' I could hear the sounds of impact connecting and the crunches and snapping of breaking bones, the grunts and moans and screams of combat. From time to time I could even feel things going past me or coming near me but each time they did, something whisked them away.

I had not finished shaping up properly and in a few seconds it was all over. I could hear a guy making choking sounds. And then Paul's voice sternly ordered, "Put the car lights on!"

The islander who was with us went and switched on the car's headlights. I had not yet recovered from the blindness caused by the high beam but that helped. Relaxing my, 'highly skilled' kamae stance, the mighty 'Zenkutsu dachi.' How do you spell dickhead? I had achieved nothing of contribution.

When the lights came on I could see that a big fat guy was being suspended against a wall, held up only by Paul's right hand on his throat, the other gripping his wrist.

In a deep interrogative voice Paul questioned, "What is going on?" The guy he was questioning, held up by the neck was not in a position to speak. All the poor fellow could do was gargle and choke.

"I repeat, what is going on? Tell me now!!" The guy being throttled was changing colour and his eyes were rolling upwards, about to lose consciousness.

Paul repeated, "Speak now!" As the guy was about to leave the planet, Paul released his grip and before he could hit the ground gave him a hard and fast slap across the face. Now if you know Paul he is a worker. By 'work' I use that term in the true meaning of the word, not a paper shuffler. A builder, fisherman and a farmer of the old tradition where we used real tools, not fancy noisy toys. The callouses on his hand are as hard as timber, the muscles behind them extremely powerful and fast; no matter what, he got the job done! I had heard that his slap was like getting hit by a plank or a baseball bat.

Paul's build would put a brick shithouse to shame and scare a bulldozer or two. He was known in the past as an angry young man, to break steel handcuffs and it took fifteen policemen with truncheons to eventually put him down after he hospitalised at least half of them. That was in the early 'bad days.' He still proudly bears the missing teeth from that incident. This does not detract from his smile in any way and women find him extremely attractive… bees to honey. In peaceful circumstances Paul is a jovial happy Buddha but when it's time to protect and defend, a wrathful deity and an unbreakable one at that.

He had hit the fat guy softly, otherwise we would have had to wait till he woke up. The miserable guy sat down and begged for his life. Paul had settled down by now. When things were safe he was always quick to forgive. "I'm not going to hurt you," he said quietly as his fire abated, "Just tell me what's going on?" Compassionate, he did not believe in doing more than what is needed to stop violence.

I noticed that it was all quiet and nobody else seemed to appear. The interrogation continued. The desperate fellow replied, "We mistook you for someone else. There is a conflict going on between the gangs. We were sure you were from the..... gang. I'm so sorry. Please forgive me. If I knew it was you Paul, you know I would not have sought to harm you…"

Paul grunted in acknowledgement or disgust at the obsequious grovelling.

"Can I offer you a lift," the fat guy begged.

"No, it's fine, we can walk," said Paul... "and you had better look after your friends."

I had been wondering about the friends. Where were they?

As I turned around in the light of the headlights there were eight or so broken unconscious bodies all bent into weird shapes that appeared to have been hit by a truck or destroyed as if by a bomb strike. Many had very evident broken bones. They looked dead to me and only three were sitting in uncomfortable positions, semiconsciously drooling and trying to breathe.

Now, I had heard about Paul's exploits as a combat warrior but what had happened here I could never have expected or believed if simply told about it. In a few seconds or less, Paul alone, had dispatched a group of attackers. So much for so-called 'martial arts,' the dancey sports I had practiced. I was really glad this man was my friend. That he was my mentor and father figure, a bonus. That place, at that time.... well, I would not have wanted to be alone in that situation!

I was to learn a great many things while apprenticed to this descendent of ancient kings of Erub, literally the Sparta of the Torres Strait where in previous times they produced impeccable multi-skilled warriors, protectors and providers.

Over the years I was fortunate that things you cannot learn inside the four walls of a little square dojo were imparted to me.

In this realm the dojo was nature and the universe!

On this night Paul had yet again dispatched a multiple attack with mythical ease not comparable to anything I had ever seen. I was a witness and yet I did not see it but for the results. This was achieved conclusively in pitch black with no visibility on a moonless night after being blinded by bright light!

For years I regretted not getting a visual, imagining that I had missed out on learning some 'technique' or another. It only recently dawned on me that was the teaching!

What it had imparted influenced both my Budo and the way that I was later to teach and it would empower my students greatly. Paradoxically this incident far outshone the relatively safe dojo 'dark training' and left its mark indelibly and for life.

Once you witness the impossible, as with the four minute mile impasse, it somehow becomes possible. It was never really beyond the bounds of possibility except in the strictures of limited thinking.

It was said that this Elder could control the sea and storm but those stories are for another time for if I told what other things I had witnessed, nobody would believe me.

4. Playing Superman

During the changes of tide whether rising or falling, the current around Thursday Island is very fast and strong. It is so strong that a motorised vessel at some times could not travel upstream against the tide.

Large and powerful motorised boats attempting to negotiate the current would go backwards instead. A sight to behold! Those that did make it against the stream travelled slower than a walk and consumed immense amounts of fuel.

Common sense would have dictated to go with the stream and around the island the other way. Maybe they were testing their engines.

The waters in the Torres Strait are most often so crystal clear that when diving you feel as if you are suspended weightless in mid air. If you did not have to come up for a breath you could easily imagine that you were levitating or when in strong currents, flying.

In between fishing trips it got quite boring for me. I don't drink, don't like pubs or the smell of them and I hate brawls. These were a predictable event and the best way to win a fight is: Do not be there! Pain free too!

Most of the guys would hit the pub and later on each other! Grievances would arise and that would lead to the inevitable arguments and punch-ups. The more pissed-up they were, the more likely they were to fight. Not interested! The more sensible ones would chase girls and that was fun but it could also lead to fights. I learnt early that women choose and that fighting over them is a waste of time. Guys only think they catch the girl. In fact women are in charge and they only let a man catch them if they decide to let him.

I would seek other forms of entertainment that would hone my skills. At times I would take off in the dinghy with an offsider and go to local waters to catch some more cray and make some ready pocket money, moonlighting as it were. I would pay the helper with a portion of my catch or cash.

But all work and no play makes Evan a dull fellow, as the saying goes.

One day some of the boys and myself discovered a remarkable possibility. We found that if we walked to Hospital Point at such times as these tides were flowing at their fastest and got into the water, we could fly to the main wharf, like the cartoon character Superman.

Seeing how long we could travel underwater holding our breath as the rapid current took us… was a lot of fun. It was safer under the water than on the surface at such times. Well, safer in some ways. We did not consider sharks or larger predators but since they left us alone perhaps they did not like the speed being dictated by water. Who knows?

We would then walk back and do it again and kept repeating this game until we got bored and went in search of other entertainment. But there was not much that could beat this flying underwater at high speeds and steering with a slight modification of a hand or wrist. Travelling a distance of about 2000 feet/600 metres or twelve times the length of an olympic pool was a cross between surfing and skydiving.

At that speed, holding breath for the distance was not a problem because each flight would not last long. The clearer the water, the more it felt as if we were really flying. It was fun! The possibility of injury never crossed our minds. We were young, fit, strong and cocky.

The thrill and excitement of skilfully dancing with nature's awesome power made us feel bigger than life.

At the end of the day we would head off to find food.

5. Magic

P aul had finally brought the boat of his choice to the Torres Strait. The Elders were impressed and curious. Sometimes Paul is a bit of a show-off, like a big kid. On this day he wanted to show them all the gadgets, the echo sounder, the radar, the radio, and all the other bits and pieces and how to use a protractor and slide rule, dividers, charts, sextant, compass and other fancy toys to navigate.

All stuff that most Islanders then knew nothing about but which they did better without the bells and whistles. They rightly paid attention to the surface maps illustrated on paper and matched them to their own multidimensionally detailed mind maps. The paper map was a good shadow reflection and they nodded in agreement.

And so he went through each and every item one at a time while the old guys gawked, really impressed and then we travelled to the very spot well known to the old guys and dropped anchor.

WOW! They were soooo impressed!

All this remarkable equipment achieving such miraculous results. One old guy exclaimed, "White man's magic!!" The others agreed and they were carrying on somewhat.

I had to walk away and hide my mirth. You may be wondering why? Well, I had observed Islanders find any spot they chose knowing where to fish and fulfil all the same functions and much much more without any equipment at all!

The map was in their mind and the navigation system was themselves.

The only equipment they needed they already had and interestingly as if by osmosis, I picked up some of those instincts and still have them. I can find a specific portion of the reef by picturing it in my mind. Equally, I can find my way in the outback but I sometimes did get lost in cities before the GPS came about and especially after, because the rules of natural commonsense do not appear to exist in the concrete jungle. Only straight lines and boxes formed by the strictured opinions of some flat minded draftsman who will often place a road where there is a deep gully and no road could possibly be built. It is the bane of all taxi drivers.

I had watched Islanders find spots without equipment every day as they had done for many thousands of years as if it were their backyard, so I don't really know what the fuss was about. The allure of a few gadgets? I do suppose that if you are navigating in unknown distant waters, of course, gadgets would be useful. But so is commonsense!

Artificiality may have its merits. Technology whether internal or external is always necessary in order to achieve an efficient result but over-reliance on gadgets can be a trap, such as people texting and driving into a tree. Real life is here if only you care to pay attention and it is worth all the gadgets in the world to capture each moment as it is!!

Some stop making love to answer the phone. That is the equivalent of a trained monkey to a bell or Pavlov's dogs. Why put down the natural in the hope that there will be the pot of gold at the end of a phone call which most often turns out to be unimportant? Having lost that moment it will not return the same. All of life is like that. Each time bubble is of immense value. Attention scattered towards distractions make you lose your goals and distant fields are too far away.

Each moment comes only once and never again. Squandered, it leaves only regrets.

Whereas some see only water or something to steal they name 'resources' and 'interests,' the Islanders saw a magnificent multidimensional life support system and a playground integrated and not separate from their own life… indeed life itself!

I still marvel at the gatherers of money beyond what's needed. Some fail and some succeed. In the end they all die. To what end? Have we made the world a better place? Today is today and will never come again.

These old guys, these masters of the ocean, for a few minutes overlooked their own totally natural magic which can achieve results even better than the gadgets! Knowing life in its essence… enables not only navigation of ocean but of life…

Since very ancient times, since many thousands of years ago, at least 50,000 years but most likely even more, before the tragically polluted panic we now call, 'civilisation' arrived; probably before even the islands came into being, people of the region have used astronomy, the Milky Way, the Stars of Tagai, their inner compass,… and Zogo to navigate the blue water empire and surrounds!

They live in the ocean, not just on it. They are the ocean!

Who has the real magic?

6. Comedy Capers

A practical and patient man and no tolerator of bullshit, Paul our fearless leader and Elder, especially when working in the sun, would tan a few shades darker than many others and this served to highlight his immense brightness of spirit.

One day, one of the guys got a bee in his bonnet and started to imagine that Paul was not going to pay us, although there was no evidence he would do other than he usually did. This fellow had been talking to a drunk at the pub. This strike was unwarranted.

Anyway, he egged-on the crew members. The imagination that they were not going to get paid progressively got worse. He wanted the money on Friday so that he could drink it through the weekend but that was not the story he was telling. So he infected the minds of the crew and generated a ludicrous 'strike' like incident.

It was a late Friday when we had offloaded to the buyers but of course the banks were shut and Paul could not pay anyone until Monday. That's just common sense and he notified the crew of this fact. Paul always paid promptly and he was generous with unexpected bonuses, striving to help his fellow Islanders.

The silliness had no basis and no real precedent.

To cut a long story short, there was a lot of bullshit and strong talk and people huddling together and then the 'hero,' the fool who expected the banks to open for him on the weekend came forward, stood up, beat his chest and made demanding noises in a loud voice.

When Paul arrived at the jetty, the agitator asserted, "We are on strike!"

Paul, taken aback, "What? What's going on?"

Paul listened patiently and when done, he set about explaining that it was Friday and the banks would not be opening until Monday and then first thing Monday, once the banks were open, he would get the pay packets and distribute them as usual. These were the days of dollar notes and coins and no pub would accept a cheque.

But no, Mr Dickhead, I forget his name, decided to push forward with his idea and rambled about industrial demands but he had none.

Paul reminded him, "You are on a break and there is nothing to do! Why don't you go and enjoy the weekend?"

The 'hero' rambled. He had been listening to a drunk at the pub expounding his version of Karl Marx. But this farce was quickly declining to Groucho, Chico, Harpo and Zeppo instead.

Again Paul listened patiently and then explained that there was no call for anything like this. He added cheekily, "You can strike as much as you want until Monday and then I'll pay you and if you want to continue working with this crew, well and good, and if not, you can go your way."

But I think the wit went over their heads.

Mind you, Paul was highly experienced at real industrial action from the days when we were cutting sugar cane by hand, negotiating better conditions for the workers. He would usually speak with the farmers and overcame through diplomacy at first and if necessary, discussion and appropriate industrial action as may have been required, always striving to achieve a win-win situation. He mostly succeeded and many of the local farmers became best friends because he was a hard worker, a powerful producer and a fair man. He was not new to striking a balance but this incident was entirely farcical.

Again he tried explaining and again Mr Dickhead raised his voice and wanted to show what a hero he was in front of all these poor fools he had beguiled.

By this time Paul was getting a bit annoyed and said, "Well I can't do anything until Monday." Paul was always striving to uplift and enrich the community and he worked hard to achieve the greater good for all. As often happens when largesse is held out, some fools will deprecate it.

Yet again the ignorant Mr Dickhead persisted in this irrational vein. I once witnessed this fellow 'fix' an outboard motor by wrapping hessian around a spark plug and belting it in with a hammer. Surprisingly, it still worked for a while which I found remarkable after he had destroyed the thread!! When it finally broke, he shouted a lot and blamed everyone but himself. This is the kind of dope he chose to be.

The ingrate Mr Dickhead decided to push harder for strike action!!! Paraphrasing his mate from the pub, "You capitalists are all the same," he called out. "Exploiting us poor black fellas…" On this boat he did not acknowledge how well off he was and then made the mistake of uttering an 'Uncle Tom' reference and other racial allusions about 'coconuts,' directed at Paul which I will not repeat.

It was unfair to level this slap-face accusation at Paul who often broke even after paying costs and wages and whose avowed mission, notwithstanding his own trials and tribulations, was to elevate his fellow Islanders!

This finally succeeded in pushing Paul's buttons, Paul seemed to expand! He usually did when he was starting to get angry.

He stood up looking larger than life and said, "You fucking ignorant black bastards, I'll pay you when I'm good and fucking ready and if that is not good enough you can piss-off now and don't ever come back," and he stormed off at a deliberate slow walk.

I had to hold it in and keep a straight face in order not to upset anyone during this very serious situation. It was only comical because Paul's skin tone, having tanned very dark from working in the sun, was the darkest of them all!! The defunct meaning had no effect other than to be somewhat ridiculous.

But I did notice the older men shrivelling at that comment as if intimidated. It's not easy to intimidate one from an ancient warrior race and at the time I did not understand the implications. Later, speaking quietly with Paul, he was feeling bad about the skin colour comment because he saw how it affected the older men who had been exploited by the invaders when they were young. That derogatory term had been used a lot by Europeans back in those days.

He settled himself down and first thing the following day made his way to the boat, sought out the Elders and apologised to them explaining that the gentleman in question had missed a few points of understanding; such as the obvious one that the banks are shut over the weekend and that he was sorry if he had upset them. That had not been his intention. Amends were made and all was good. They were not fools and understood.

Dickhead was still storming around angrily and gossiping around town entirely oblivious to the sacrifices Paul and others like him had made and are still making to intercede against real racism and oppression in order to bring opportunity to the Islands.

The labourer being worthy of his reward, as always, spot on time the following Monday the crew got paid promptly and early shortly after the bank opened.

The sensible ones bought essentials for their families. The others, miserable at having to spend a weekend sober, begrudgingly accepted payment.

How they spent their wages on that day remains unknown.

7. Find Out First

Lui had the kindest heart in the world. He saved my life once and probably didn't even realise it. His head sometimes missed a beat but his heart was gold. A good honest person, sometimes his vivid imagination would get away and he convinced even the best of those who did not know him better… of the impossible.

Sometimes his antics would lead to silly outcomes and then, well, it was not always appreciated.

Some people who knew him considered Lui to be a half-wit but I did not think so. He was different. A person is entitled to be different. The problem is this, Lui was not fluent in social graces and smooth interaction but for his wildest make-believe imagination…

From a powerful ancestry his appearance was very dignified until he overdid it and got caught out bullshitting. He could weave and spin the b.s. like a master craftsman and a true artist.

Being there was an experience. I think it was at Yam Island that he made an inappropriate comment about a girl. Lui never made such comments because he was a gentleman at heart but he had been associating with hoods at T.I. and had been parroting their behaviours, hoping to gain acceptance from the crew. 'Big man' bullshit and all that.

Unbeknownst to Lui, the girl's mother was standing right next to him at the time he made the comment. Faux-pas big time! Well, he succeeded in ruining community relations for our boat crew.

Mum took a stick to Lui and beat the shit out of him. Paul asked us to stand back and let him learn from his mistake by experience. After all it was a relatively safe situation. Poor Lui copped a token hiding that day. The small mum could not have physically hurt him but the public humiliation left its mark, hopefully offering a lesson in social graces.

He found out the hard way! Despite our remonstrations and apologies that incident soured relations and caused embarrassment to us.

We had to leave!

That evening on the boat, anchored outside instead of being accommodated ashore as had been the original plan, Paul explained to us an important principle of life. This being: In all things; FIND OUT FIRST!

Especially when you are in unknown territory or a new situation, find out first. Find out where you are. Find out who you are with. Find out the relations. Find out the safety factors. Find out security. Find out the customs etiquette, protocols, expected behaviours, rules, pros, cons… and of course who is who! Find out everything that you possibly can and then some! Most importantly in the ocean before jumping into the water!

He then told us a story: One time when he was in New Guinea he was not able to find out what it was that he was expected to be eating and he chose to break the social etiquette in relation to offered food. In doing so he ran the risk of being killed. He had to leave in an immense hurry or they would have cut him up for the insult that he had extended to them. Sneaking out unnoticed he bolted without saying goodbye….

In the customs of the Melanesian region it is an insult to refuse food. There are many ramifications and implications and other tribal people throughout the world have similar ways which once had purpose. The refusal of food offered is not only seen as bad manners against the effort expended in acquiring that food but as an implication that you assume that the food may be poisoned. This is taken as the supreme insult! Even though, similar to corporate business dealings, it may well sometimes be poisoned!!

In New Guinea this may lead to serious consequences when enraged tribal people become emotional. In this case the food was dubious and he didn't know what it was! Being a sensitive eater and finding himself in cannibal country he did not want to take that chance.

Making the effort to find out enables a better navigation of life and everything else. When you find out as much as possible you'll be less likely to come to harm or to hurt people or to insult people or ruin relations. In the ocean you will decrease the chances of being eaten!

Paul's efforts to make diplomatic amends over Lui went down like cold porridge. Not well. This wound would take some time to heal. We had lost face and had to leave trying not to feel ashamed for Lui's action.

The sad thing was that Lui was not the type of guy to make that kind of comment. He was mimicking other idiots and trying to look heroic and it backfired for all of us. Not a good ambassador!

Another time Lui ran the boat onto the reef when he fell asleep day-dreaming on top of the mast and missed giving navigation signals to the guy on the bow who would match the signal to the man at the wheel. It was serious teamwork with consequences. We usually piloted the reef like this because direct visual was more reliable than the gadgets. Well, that is provided the man on the mast was awake!

With Lui on the mast we would soon find out what these consequences were.

The man on the mast was the main lookout everyone placed their reliance upon as he could see the depths and channels clearly. This method required the usually three man team to remain focussed and on the ball when piloting reefs.

Grounded on top of a reef, we had to wait for the tide to come up. Always at the ready and capitalising on any given situation, Paul arranged that we scrape the barnacles off the bottom of the boat while we were high and dry in the descending tide. When the water finally came up a little we pushed and tilted the boat over onto the other side and scraped the barnacles off that side in time before the full tide released the mother boat.

Some idiot whinged that this was not the work that they wanted to do. It was to trigger the rancour that would later lead to the so-called 'strike' incident by Mr Stupid later on, when we landed at T.I. on a Friday.

We did not have antifouling paint with us but that would be the task when we arrived back at Thursday Island. Then the boat would go up onto the slipway where we would finish the cleaning to a fine level and paint the boat hull with antifouling, leaving it to dry.

In a sense Lui had done us a favour.

Understanding Lui's condition, Paul never even bothered getting angry but he did let him know, full well risking that his words would most likely go in one ear and out of the other. He told him anyway hoping that some would land on fertile soil.

This one tops it: During a crew shortage, Paul left Lui in charge of the mother boat until we all returned.

Lui sold Paul's trawler for a bargain basement price in Paul's absence! Yup! Not a typo.

Having recently observed negotiations for a boat sale at Thursday Island, he had somehow memorised the technique and unleashed it on an unsuspecting visitor who happened to comment that he liked our boat.

Once the b.s. began to flow, Lui could not contain himself and he convinced the passerby that he owned the boat and that it was for sale; and somehow negotiated an offer and acceptance. Lui asked for cash and arranged a rendezvous point for the exchange.

When the man came to collect and pay, Paul was there!

"Well who are you?" asked the wealthy buyer.

"Who are *you*?!!" remonstrated Paul.

Following a strong discussion Paul explained that he was the true owner of the boat.

"I don't believe you. You can't be. The owner has sold me the boat," said the now confused, acquisitional entrepreneur who really badly wanted to claim the bargain he had scored.

"I am the owner and I can show you the papers," said Paul, slightly miffed. After some words and catching the drift of what had happened, Paul didn't really need to explain but made it clear anyway, "The guy who pretended to be the owner is a half wit and he is not in any way authorised to sell the boat because he has no rights of tenure. Please leave!"

More strong talk followed. In fact a major stoush ensued before the explanations were accepted and the matter was corrected. At first the prospective buyer then wanted Lui charged for fraud but Paul sweet talked him and he left, having become Paul's best friend.

Mind you Lui was not on drugs or anything. He was stone cold sober when his brain was doing funny things as it often did.

If Paul was angry he managed to hide it somewhat. Despite the potential for serious consequences the situation was sort of funny but only because Paul's diplomatic skill caused strong emotions to be soothed.

Heavy hearted and with immense compassion, Paul sacked the young man, delivering an explanation that this is the sort of thing that is not done.

As far as I know Paul never employed Lui again but out of compassion gave him a sizeable bonus to pass on to his family to help them along. He could not afford to have Lui around because of the damage that he sometimes did.

To Lui's credit, to his immense credit, he saved my life during a knife attack a year and a half earlier *(See Book 3*

- 'Queensland CLOSE SHAVES 'Nobody Beats Me in The Kitchen.') so he wasn't entirely the half wit people said.

Maybe the poor dude had once been traumatised and had become a daydreamer.

I understood!

8. Message

I was there. This happened at either Saim or Mogor village at Erub. We were visiting some of Paul's relatives. As I recall, we had lunch and we were sitting around talking.

This was before most islands got airports. Maybe Masig had an airfield then, it's been a long time.

It was a still, fine day. Not even a breeze was stirring and the water was so motionless that at a glance you could have mistaken it for a solid surface. You could almost reach out and touch the stillness. The atmosphere had an electric air of unity about it.

An old man was sitting, apparently sleeping or meditating in a small palm frond humpy shading him from the sun.

Suddenly he appeared to awaken and approached us, "Passi sends word that a girl at Mer has broken her arm and hit her head. She's unconscious and needs urgent medical attention. You need to get her to the hospital at Thursday Island fast."

The Melbidir supply ship would not be coming for a week or more and this ambulance transport would have to be conducted urgently by anyone with a fast boat. The nearest fast boat was on another island and we had to get to it. A young lady had fallen off a palm tree whilst picking coconuts.

We prepared a dinghy and provisions to make a fast trip there and see what we could arrange.

Twenty minutes later, as we were about to launch and go, the 'white man school teacher' from on top of the hill came running down screaming orders, "Stop what you're doing right now, forget about it. I just got a radio telegraph from the school teacher at Murray Island saying that a girl has fallen off a tree and broken her arm and she's in a bad way and needs to go to the hospital. Stop what you're doing right now, change your plan. You must go to Murray Island instead…"

With an almost imperceptible tone of sarcasm Paul jokingly quipped, "Yassa master.. Will do as you say!" as he had heard negro slaves in black-and-white movies from America speaking to the slave masters.

How could we possibly explain to the four eyed academic that we had already received a message by a superior, faster means than clunky slow gadgets and that we were ahead of the game.

We continued to dispatch the crew who then took her on a round trip to nearby Masig Island where somebody there had a speed boat.

She got to Thursday Island hospital in record time.

9. Bommie

Anchored south-west of Mer following a successful day we were enjoying a break and a well earned feed. Relaxing over a late lunch, refrigerator full, it was the end of this trip. The ocean was so glazen calm it looked oily.

The course was set and we would at any moment weigh anchor and head for Thursday Island.

This happened: As usual, our fishing trip had been well executed and we were preparing to return to offload our catch. From our safe distance we watched the giant breakers pounding the Great Barrier Reef as they had done for many thousands or perhaps even millions of years.

The catch had been good.

We were in a broad expanse of clear water near a forest of bommies. To the east of us, on the horizon, we could see the giant waves at the edge of the barrier spraying high into the air. To our west were the bommies.

Over lunch Paul was telling tales about visiting Yampi Sound off the northern coast of Western Australia where he had worked with the Japanese cultivating pearls at Broome and about his stopover at Darwin in the Northern Territory. As it usually does in nature, especially when undisciplined fools, drunks and smart arses with no common sense are about, the unplanned happened!

When the air is as still as it was on this fine day, you can hear for miles and we thought we were hearing singing.

One of the crew was keeping watch and it was not long before a vessel appeared on the horizon drifting our way at speed in the tidal current that had turned from the west now travelling eastwards.

From the caterwauling it was obvious that drunks were doing the singing. This was no place for the inebriated and it was not long before they came our way being impelled uncontrollably towards the Great Barrier Reef where they would have been smashed and torn to pieces, pulped into matchsticks, broken bones and fish food.

As they approached we could see the idiots, two white men and one islander whom they had no doubt co-opted from the T.I. pub. They were visibly as drunk as skunks. Between them they were not only useless and dangerous to themselves but unqualified to be out at sea. Worse, being so badly intoxicated it was a foregone conclusion that without intervention they were already dead.

The ocean is a dangerous mistress.

They were being carried at considerable speed towards the edge of the great reef barrier where very deep water meets a shallow reef surface, an immensely powerful washing machine that decimates everything which is drawn into it.

We realised that we would have to place ourselves at risk to save their lives. It was not a decision that out of humanity we could other than make. As it was, in this case these were the lives of suicidal fools totally out of touch with reality.

Quickly we weighed anchor.

Moving away from our safe spot, pulling up alongside them we called out, "Give us a rope, you are in danger…" The most arrogant drunk, presumably the unlicensed skipper, rambled incoherent garbage, "Fuck off, we're having fun! We'll see where the tides take us. We're following our dream… our destiny… you never know what island paradise and women… the tide will take us…" and other shit like that. Maybe they had been imbibing more than only alcohol!

Fun indeed! They were drifting towards certain death. Paul tried to appeal to reason but reason was not prevailing. There was not much time to take action or we would have to let them go to their fate in order not to place ourselves at irretrievable risk.

He then appealed to the islander who was with them.

Although drunk he would hopefully better understand. "Throw us a line, Paul called out, "We can tow you!" The white guy again said, "Just fuck off, we don't need any help…" He was so smashed that he was worthy of ignoring.

"They gonna sack me if I don't do what I'm told," called the islander who was with them.

"You're dead if you do," shouted Paul. "You're heading towards the barrier!!"

We managed to tow them to safe waters and give them some fuel, which they had run out of because of bad planning or no planning at all… Pointing them in the right direction and giving them strict orders to head back home, we left them to their own devices.

We had better plans than to babysit these fools and the rescue had placed us closer to risky waters.

This saga had taken a fair while of unplanned time and we were now at a disadvantage. The day was ending. We had lost the best timing for turning home in daylight and as dusk fell an impending storm was beginning to escalate. The increasing surges were posing high risk. In order to save them we had gone past the bommie field and the same tide that we rescued them from was now impelling us towards the bommies.

We were now in unsafe waters. It was too late to get out. It was fast getting darker, too dark to safely negotiate this vast minefield of coral outcrops. The tidal current had previously created a risk of getting smashed on the barrier reef. Now that tide was presenting the new risk of being driven towards a greater unpredictable risk, first the bommie field and if we survived that, then the Great Barrier Reef in the night! We had virtually exchanged places with the fools we had saved and found ourselves in an even worse situation. That can sometimes be the price you pay. Not good!

A bommie is a skyscraper of hard coral growing out of deep water. Sometimes these column-like protrusions are visible from the surface but not always. Depending on the tide, when under the surface, bommies pose immense risk for navigators.

In the rising storm the waves were lifting us up and down and navigation was by sheer skill and intuition. At any moment we could have been smashed onto a bommie and that would have been the end of us. Having no choice than to try, we fought hard and fast to anchor the mother boat before entering into extraordinary risk.

The ocean here was too deep for the long chain and rope to find the bottom so we put down onto the nearest bommie hoping to hold beside it before being swept into the thicker accumulation which would have produced even greater risk. The chance we were taking was to aim to stay in between the bommies on all sides.

It was quite possible that we could have easily swung around and smashed into one but Paul knew what he was doing. From a lifetime of experience he understood local conditions and he made a call.

Suddenly it was night and the waves had grown gigantic. I always laugh at the amateurs in Sydney Harbour when the sea gets a little choppy or there is a bit of a swell and they call it, 'rough.' That's not anywhere near rough.

We were now being pounded into the depths and thrown into the heights again and again. Valleys and mountains of raging waters. Up and down, up and down, up and down relentlessly amid gigantic waves which would persist all night long but not before a thunderstorm added itself to the unfolding rage.

With each spectacular explosion the now black waters and sky lit up bright silver-blue each time thunder flashed and lightning struck the ocean nearby.

It was truly magnificent!

Most of the crew hid in the berths below deck. A form of denial I thought and I found this surprising for people with ancestry such as theirs. The Elders were in the wheelhouse with Paul and me confronting the storm. Facing risk is always best!

At first we made tea and silently drank it in that rollercoaster of death, rolling swaying and smashing back down into the sea, holding our balance each time the boat pounded down... juggling our mugs trying not to spill our hot drinks. At the mercy of the elements there was nothing else we could do than to wait it out.

I don't think anyone down below really slept.

My good friend lightning was speaking to me.

Needing to go outside to urinate overboard as you do on a boat, I gingerly shuffled onto the side deck.

Overboard was virtually indistinguishable and in the wind and spray the piss was going everywhere. It was as quickly washed away. Drenched and hanging on strongly I did my thing, then on a whim decided to face it in full. After all if we were going to die I may as well meet eternity with a clear mind.

Gripping the bulwark at each pause I cautiously made my way over that slippery deck to the bow. Those in the wheelhouse could do nothing about it. They must have thought me mad. Tightly grasping the bow rope, facing the storm I stood there in only swim shorts riding the movement as the boat rose high into the air and then sunk deep into the black pits of darkness then back up and then down again continuously. The high wind ferociously chilling, stinging beads of rain cutting into my skin, my hair on end… witnessing!

On the razor edge of life and death I experienced a mystically deep intensely vivid bliss!

From a greater height all this is nothing. From a puny mortal view, everything! When there is no choice, face death willingly and it may not take you. A force greater than myself made me immensely calm on the inside. It was terribly violent outside but intensely beautiful in a way not easy to describe. You could feel the awesome presence of an almighty power which was simultaneously wrathful and yet peaceful. As if standing in the presence of the Divine, it bathed through me with its awesome electric fury each time lightning struck…I became… any moment… any moment… each moment was a MOMENT… RIGHT NOW!!!

For a long timeless time I stood holding on like this, witnessing and dynamically riding the violent undulations, enjoying the majesty of this once-in-a-lifetime event.

We could have been dashed upon one of the coral outcrops and killed but life was so imminent and powerful that the ocean was going to decide our fate, not us mortals.

I could not do anything other than commune with it.

Live or die what does it matter… it was more real than real. At rare opportunities like this you realise that death is an illusion and that all the power of the Universe is present in and all around us all the time and that life as we think we know it.. is just a dream.

Blinding flashes of silver-blue ignited the surrounding clouds for an instant and then it was pitch black again. After a pause… again…BANG! BOOM! repeating and after each pause blinding light! And again! Then again and again this dance of the eternal thunders prevailed!

Without warning the anchor suddenly pulled out and we were adrift, snapping me out of my reverie.

I was in the right place!

When a boat drifts it no longer sways from the bow to the stern but from side to side. This causes a sleeping seaman to awaken. Paul and those in the wheelhouse had not been sleeping. Almost immediately Paul started the engine at full throttle against the current and signalled to me.

Knowing his intent, I was already in position to hoist anchor and did so. As fast as I could, holding my sea legs against the weight balancing as only the ocean can teach… Anchor up…

He somehow intuited another bommie on which to cast anchor again in the midst of that storm.

He signalled again. I could barely see him through the thick rain. I let it drop. He had managed to steer without crashing…

It did not hold! Again I cast. It failed and I had to haul it in. Someone came out to help me. Yet again it proved a slip and with burning muscles we had to haul again. And again. It took four attempts in that dark. The last time it held fast.

I got myself back into the wheelhouse. I could have no longer stood safely on that bow this time around. The storm was resurging to a greater height and nature rearing her wrath!

It was now not possible to boil water to make tea. The ocean was boiling outside and the waves were now crashing and tossing the boat around like a cork and the cooking stove pot restraints would not have been sufficient to hold steady. Anything left loose was flying around. We let anything not battened down go where it would. It was too late to fiddle.

After that, a new alertness prevailed among the crew. They all knew the possibility of our imminent fate.

Maelstrom… waves smashing over the top of the wheelhouse. It could have been the end. Holding fast, the crew took turns on the bilge pump bailing frantically. The rest sat quietly staring silently ahead, as if in deadly meditation… primeval ancients sullenly communing within the bowels of primordial soup…

Ages passed. Time stood still as if forever... Waiting, waiting, waiting patiently for change.... or death! It was a long night... Until dawn.

As swiftly as it had begun what seemed so long ago, the storm abated.

Then the inevitable... Timeless time... With the coming of the light of morning the dark faded away as if it had never been... the waves settling... the clouds were no more to be seen and all was still.

The brilliant sun rose unobstructed into the glowing horizon and pure blue sky. It was as if all of that magnificent fury had never happened. A dream. A very real dream. Eternity held in a moment and passing in a night.

In silence and in clarity we headed back towards T.I., the MV 'Ina' cutting through a now calm and peaceful sea.

The fresh salty breeze stung our nostrils pleasantly as the glowing sun bathed us with comforting warmth, glittering the smooth ocean behind us, disturbed only by the wake the boat left behind.

Another day in the Torres Strait.

10. Three-Zero-Three

Even though I had seen white pointer sharks easily dispatched using a point 303 rifle, I did not then know that the military issue caliber .303 was one of the few guns that could be lethal if shooting at something through water.

Apparently the speed is just right. Modern fast guns shatter the bullet or the water slows it down and the projectile does not arrive at the target. When I saw the science of this demonstrated in a TV documentary years later my hair stood on end at how close a close shave I had had.

On this fine day I was sitting on the stern of the MV 'Ina,' a 45 foot prawn trawler which was moored at the end of the jetty, chatting with Sammy Lakon. A young woman had just turned up. She was trying to hide from Mark the abuser who was bothering her.

I had made a fresh pot of tea and prepared fried scones with jam. We were enjoying them in the warm winter sun.

Some ten minutes later Mark, drunk, drugged and violent approached.

Hiding behind Sammy the girl asked for our protection.

"You bastards are fucking her.. "Mark snarled jealously accusing without introduction.

Hoping to de-escalate the situation Sammy tried talking some sense but his obsequious tone served to make things worse, "We're only sitting here talking…"

"Have some tea and scones.." I suggested, hoping to put a dampener on the violence which was brewing.

Ignoring me, Mark berated the girl, "You fucken' slut.."

"I barely know you," she pleaded, "We only met recently and I don't want you."

That did it. Grabbing her by the hair, Mark began to slap her. Without a pause old Sammy stepped in. A punch-up ensued and Sammy's right eye brow was split open about three inches from one of the hard, bare knuckle punches Mark had thrown. Old Sam was weak from years of alcohol and metho abuse and being a coward and a lowlife, Mark was quite at ease with slapping and abusing women, children and old people.

Exploding, I stepped in, "Go now!!" I said calmly punching Mark in the face about twenty or so times. The punches were focussed and hard. Outraged at the behaviour of this mongrel I wanted him away. I may as well have been punching a car tyre. Nothing happened. Islanders are unbelievably strong.

Unable to outbox me, he reached out and gripped my throat trying to tear it out.

From my training, I tucked my chin down and applied a Hiji Jime kansetsu waza, an effective arm breaker he had walked himself into and it would have worked well had I some flat ground behind me. Instinctively he countered strongly by pushing hard with his whole bodyweight behind him to stop his arm snapping. The railing caught me behind the knees and we went overboard struggling for control.

I planned to use aquatic Newaza techniques and test who had the longest lungs. He smoked and drank and I didn't. It could have drowned the son-of-a-bitch and I would resuscitate him afterward but he sure was not going to harm anyone on my watch! And he knew it…

The struggle was futile and the slippery bastard got loose. With an explosion of energy he leapt away swimming towards the boat and I could not hang onto him. He had rubbed himself with coconut oil and in the water a person becomes even more slippery as a result.

I knew he was going for the rifle.

Being closer to the trawler than me, he got there first and clambered aboard. Conundrum!

It would be too slow to follow him. Climbing up after him would be risky and I knew that if I did, it would be at very high risk of getting kicked or bashed on the head with something. Or shot!

He emerged from the wheelhouse with the gun aiming in my direction. Taking a hurried breath I submerged fast. There was no time to hyperventilate. I didn't have that luxury but my exploding adrenals compensated for the lack of air. I would have to rely on anaerobic fitness for backup. By the way, as an aside, the method of submerging you see in the movies of amateurs sticking their arse up in the air is not the way it's done. In this case it would have been shot off. I submerged in the proper manner instead, straight down.

I began to swim towards the shore under the water, before realising that it was a bad move because it was unlikely I would get out of range fast enough without having to emerge for breath. Once on the surface, if even briefly, I would have been a target and could have worn a bullet in the head.

I found myself in a very high risk position that needed to be changed ASAP, about 40 metres from the boat with the shore about 250 metres away.

In deep water? Well the water was not really that deep! Only a couple of fathoms, maybe three. More like deep shit proverbially speaking. On the shore there were slipways and other buildings. People there were too far away to witness anything much and in the islands in those days, especially Thursday Island, violence was not uncommon. People did not give a damn and did not usually want to be involved, unless of course it was their relatives, in which case it would turn into a small war. More often than not, people tended to look the other way.

Having to move fast, I had gone under without breath preparation. I needed to come up for air. Urgently!!!

He didn't know where I was and kept shooting at a relentless pace. A Vietnam veteran, many considered him a fuckup. He was a known drunk, a self confessed child molester, a sadist and rapist and his bad habits had followed him home. Including deadly violence. A very lost soul and a scourge to those weaker than him. Especially when on drugs and alcohol, he became possessed and out of control. A well formed and good looking fellow but a high risk danger to others. He would too often use those looks to charm and lure his victims.

Peppering the waters in what he thought was my direction… under water tracers sped past me on all sides… Fast white bubbles….

None came closer than a foot or so. In other words he missed!

In hindsight I imagine some harm could have been done but at the time I was too busy surviving to give it a thought.

Nolens volens, finally having to surface for breath again, I waited for a pause where he would be reloading or searching for more bullets or watching for me to emerge! I could not know which it would be and so I had to guess! The tracers stopped. I paused a little.

It was a longer interval. This would have to be it!

Lungs bursting, I had no choice than to resurface, just in time to see him dart into the wheelhouse.

Fortuitous good timing it was.

His appearance had taken on that of a hateful devil. I still don't know why he disliked me so much. This was not the first incident with this demon and it would not be the last.

In an instant I knew what to do. Breathing fast and repeatedly while he was looking for more bullets, I took as many deep breaths as possible before diving again the moment I saw him returning.

He came out reloading quickly then started shooting again but in those few seconds that it took, before he could take aim, I was out of sight along the muddy bottom leaving those white bubbles behind…

Swimming hard and fast along the ocean floor, this time I made towards the boat. Towards the shooter. It was strategically preferable and nearer than the shore… only 40 metres or so. It would have been an easy task but for the increased adrenal stress. A short distance but more than enough considering the situation.

Better prepared this time, the journey underwater was not so bad. Hugging the seabed it took less than a minute. A quick flashback of doing the length of swimming pools under the water as a kid passed my mind's eye. It calmed me and lent focus.

I got there.

At the boat, I passed under it and surfaced seaward. Holding on to the side and listening, I took deep long recovery breaths as quietly as possible. The reports of the rifle shooting from the opposite side of the boat could still be heard.

It is strange the things that you notice in passing during emergency situations. I recall the barnacles under the boat and thinking that it was about time it went up on the slipway for a clean... But that thought was over quickly. I had an immediate and urgent situation to take care of.

Waiting long enough to quickly catch my breath, I climbed atop the wheelhouse above him and observed the situation. He was still shooting and looking at the water where he thought I was.

He didn't know I was standing above him. As he relaxed resting the gun barrel upward, on top and behind him I took hold of it snatching it out of his hands hard and fast. The barrel was hot. Flipping it around I pointed it at his head in one move.

The look of surprise and fear was priceless.

"I'll count to ten and then you're dead!" I growled.

I've never seen a coward leave a trail of shit running so fast!

I dutifully counted to ten, after all a promise is a promise, except that I did not say how fast I was going to count. In this case very fast. I wanted to frighten some sense into him so I pointed the damn killing implement towards the sky and pulled the trigger.

"Click," the magazine was empty.

Damn! How I would have loved to see how high he would jump at the sound of the discharge. But it was not to be. Making like the Road Runner he was soon out of sight!

Is it not so very interesting how heroes prove themselves to be cowards when the tables are turned?

After hiding the gun by tucking it into a difficult to find position in the engine room, I drove the girl home on the other side of T.I., then Sammy to hospital for stitches and made my way to the police station to report the incident.

"You look alright to us," they said, "No bullet holes…," and went back to watching television.

I had a dark tan back then.

Another day at the isles of despair. Tomorrow would bring new extremes. Good? Bad? Indifferent? Who could know? Each day was new and that's the way it was!

Many years later I read, *"There is nothing more exhilarating than to be shot at with no result."*

Winston, I understand!

11. Incline

Bored with the wait while the other crew were out drinking, I decided to go fish. One of the locals heard me planning out loud and offered to row the dinghy for me. I agreed to pay him a portion of the catch. Out we went. There are some good reefs near Thursday Island.

Free diving for crayfish just east of T.I., the more I travelled along the ocean floor the more there were and the larger they got.

Enthralled, I decided to follow the catch zone.

The incline was subtle. I should have listened to the still small voice of warning but the possibility of wads of dollars kept me going. With the long fins I had recently purchased secondhand from a young man who was leaving the islands, I thought I had the advantage.

In those days I had three minute lungs and five minutes in an emergency. There were occasions that those two minutes of reserve would save my life.

This was to be such a day.

Captivated with the possibility I was witnessing, I had been travelling along the floor for quite some time. Suddenly, my inner warning triggered me to go up for air.

I turned upwards but when I expected to reach the surface, the surface was not there.

Another minute gone, I kicked again.

Still no surface.

My fifth minute gone I realised what had happened. I sent a quick invocation and kicked like all hell.

I blacked out.

I awoke kicking so hard I was rising up to my waist. I recall coming to as I surfaced. The dinghy boy was astounded.

He had thought me dead.

In shock I gathered my composure, "Fuck it!" I spat out, "We're going home. Day off!!"

I sold the few cray we had, gave the boy his portion of the cash and some of the other fish I had caught to take to his family. It was not as much as I had planned but it was good pocket money.

The realisation? Breath is worth more than all the money in the world.

12. Dance Feast

After living under the universe, under the Milky Way and the Stars of Tagai where the power of nature was directly and abundantly with us without reservation, I finally had to return to Sydney, that grey concrete jungle of bleak where everyone is individually and unrepentantly subsisting in sterile square boxes made of ticky tacky and chasing after money before they die.

No stars, instead smog. No crystal clear air but pollution. No silence, only noise, cacophony and discord. No clarity of consciousness but lots of desperate monkey mind chattering in conflict of opinions. When beings know no better they consider enslavement as normal and dare not dream. No freedom to soar, only masses of repetitive drone habits and depression. No thriving, only standardised, lobotomised struggle in denial. Plastic semblances of happiness found in substances that wear out. No inclusive, warm consciousness, only cold separate clinging to debt and fear of loss… never looking up at the universe and all its glories, eyes fixated on the ground, prisoners to manufactured lack...a dark corner of existence lit up by wasteful fireworks once a year and then the daily drudging race against time everyone loses in the end.

It was a totally different dimension to that which I had experienced in Island Life. By comparison it was a taste of hell. Having reclaimed my soul in clean air, deep inner calm and total Nature; so called 'civilisation,' artificiality and pollution was a hard blow to my system. Having left dynamic living reality for this lesser, shrunken existence, future-shock set in and it took some recovering.

Even with the sometimes high risk vagaries of storm and weather, life in the islands is a continual dance and feast, a celebration of life and not a desperation of strife. This is not to say that like everywhere else there are not good people, bad people and all the other varieties but the attitude, the values, the outlook on life is considerably more alive and present. Nature repairs and sustains you, whereas concrete jungle cannot.

Notwithstanding invasion, the high integrity traditional core values bequeathed by the Ancient Ones had never left. When I was there, social capital and the economy of life prevailed. Communication, counsel, seeking advice from elders, learning the traditions, practical thriving skills of farming, hunting, gathering, protection, caring, nurturing, maintaining, creative skills, community bonding, natural law are better learnt here than in any university, rather directly from the universe, mother nature and those traditions which have survived the ages since before the great flood in the cultures that were then dominant.

This was evident in the immense ability to manifest abundance, even in the face of manufactured lack. Despite the more recent history of tyranny and pillage that had been visited upon this place and its people, no one was ever frightened of work. Very few shirked. They understood well that life and tomorrow depended upon the right effort of today.

Inclusively, every now and again there would be a purposeful feast and a dance, a celebration of life. No ostensible reason, rather simply for the sake of it. On special occasions that would also happen but then again, each and every moment of every day is treated as a special occasion.

In this I witnessed and participated: When work had to be done there were no begrudging attitudes, no bitching, bickering or complaining. While the men hunted, it being more risky to bring home food, the women and those who stayed behind prepared the 'cupmari' ground ovens where much of the cooking was to take place, as well pots of curry, sop-sop, rice and other goodies to accompany unbelievable variety not seen in supermarkets or fruit shops of cities.

The once copious abundance of oceanic foods is now endangered. Dugong, turtle and other staples, previously plentiful, were no longer as easy to find.

Teamwork here is an unspoken way of life! The goal came together almost effortlessly as if by magic, without struggle and without any drama. To build a boat or a house, repair the fish traps or clean the gardens.... or anything else, volunteer team work prevailed.

The cultural difference stood out dramatically. Unlike the self-obsessed, acquistionally afflicted squalor of city life where fair-weather friends abandon you when you move house or any event where there is unpaid work to be done, here, joyfully and either silently or joking and singing, everyone chipped in, including children and the disabled. Nobody shirked in those days and work was not seen as a chore or a four letter word, but fun!

When the hunters came back, all was prepared and the cooking was ready to begin. The dancing and joking and laughing and feasting and loving continued throughout the night...

All this without electricity in those days, without refrigerators in those days, without gas cooking stoves in those days, without proper sewage in those days and without so many things that city people take for granted. Here it was abundance, absolute hygiene and power without cost, food without storage and everything done with natural resources, innovation and remarkable skill in the midst of a time of poverty. Resourcefulness!

Later with the advent of sugar, other toxins and certain accommodations, it seemed to be changing the great way and many here began to mimic the life of desperation and money worship beyond its natural value as do those poor souls who line up in traffic jams in their 'freedom machines,' breathing toxins all their life for the privilege of indentured slaving in a square box all week long.

Kerosene pressure lamps and cooking stoves were a third world condescension at best but they did the job and these alterations were not subject to electricity outages, sometimes kerosene shortages but then the perennial driftwood would provide wood for fire.

The world seems to have lost or forgotten that today is today and the journey is the way and nature in her immense generosity provides endless abundance when our focus is in the right place and we protect our environments instead of allowing pillaging desecration and extraction from the life support systems of the planet in exchange for dead money and things which we leave behind when we die!

Yes but… when thinking with our butt we create misery and pollution. In the islands in those days there was no industry of pollution to vitiate the atmosphere… no flat line air conditioning, simply-natural shade, pure, ionised sea breeze and the ocean. So much sweeter and nourishing to the soul!

It has always been known that the Journey is the way and today is today. The universe is here and nature is willing to provide when we alter our values to be true… and align with the axis at the core of existence.

Perhaps if we lessened our hubris and attachment to gadgets, we may learn a thing or two from the First Peoples! It may be, it just may be that the journey between birth and death is about improving the quality of our consciousness and not the collecting of things we will be leaving behind at death!

13. Giant Stingray

Speaking of strikes, one day the boat cook went on strike, namely me, because the guys would not clean up after themselves or wash their food bowls and utensils. They began getting pushy, imagining the cook's job to be somehow that of a menial.

The crew started dumping a pile of dirty dishes after eating, expecting that I would clean up behind them. Like 30 or more!! Come on?! These things happen when young guys work together and they've got nothing better to occupy their minds. A contest of egos.

I drew the line and an angry crew threatened to throw me overboard

I said, "Go for it, I'll take my dinghy and go home. One of you will end up having to cook and you won't be eating so well any more... and they knew it!" That worried them because many young men are so used to being baby-sat by a woman, be it their mother, wife or their girlfriend, that they are somewhat challenged in the kitchen.

Although that tradition of team-working was well founded in survival efficiency in older times, latter day people took it for granted without understanding the principle behind it. When an Islander goes to catch fish or hunt there is no guarantee whether he will come back alive. Storm, shark, high risk at sea... many of the younger generation... good friends who had avoided traditional apprenticeship were lost at sea and never seen again.

And so, unlike the 'liberated' glass-ceiling chasers of the cities, Island women joyfully cook and that thankfully because they will be the ones to live and produce the next generation. However, a warrior who cannot prepare food is only half a man because it's not always possible to return home the same day!

Paul interceded to make the peace and the gentlemen decided to wash their own dishes after that. Mind you, this cook was also catching dinner, so his time was of the essence and the cook can cook better when you don't dump a lazy mess on him!

Here's a great secret of life, shirking takes a hell of a lot of effort and simply doing the job means it's over and done with and life is happy.

"Gaka nakariklu Usiami gab ge a Segi gab ge." When everyone cleans up behind themselves life flows best.

I've known the greatest of warriors to take charge of a kitchen and cook better than a gourmet chef and if not feed the multitudes, then at least lovingly feed their family without reservation of any kind!

On this particular day, I took time out from work to play with those big grey sharks that sleep on the sea bottom.

They are fun to ride.

Grabbing them by the main fin, a kick on the side and they take off. I don't know what it is about young men and speed. Anyway, I had paused from one of these rides to investigate a small cave. I stuck my head down the hole only to be confronted face to face by a Wobbegong waving its head from side to side, no doubt as startled as I was.

It kept lunging at me then retreating. I think it felt trapped. It looked like one of those monsters from Sesame Street and it was so cartoonish and unexpected that I bumped my head on the ledge above me when I recoiled backwards as it came for me and my diving mask came off.

Vision is not as clear without goggles so I decided to go back to the dinghy and reset.

I was curious. I surfaced, cleaned my goggles, replaced them and went back to see what the hell had accosted me.

All of a sudden the war of the worlds emerged as giant UFO's hovered above me casting huge shadows. About five or six of them flying above me. And then another lot. Each one as big as a house. A really hard adrenaline kick…. and then when my wind began to run out I noticed that they were giant stingrays… which ignored me and got on with their life and travels.

They happily went past and kept going and flowing effortlessly… majestically… gently as if flying ever so smoothly… they were so big! Not quite sure, I stayed down until they had all passed.

That was enough for one day, so I decided to go back to the dinghy. Then, on second thoughts, I decided to go back to the boat… maybe these were warning signs.

Yeah, too many close shaves in one day and you're tempting fate, at least that's how I felt. When there's a string of disputes you don't stick around to find out what the next one will do. It might eat you!

When I got back to the boat, the Islanders teased me. "You could've been abducted you know. Once they grab you with those big side hooks you're gone." It was all in jest.

Giant stingrays don't generally do any harm unless you attack them.

Had I not seen them for myself, I would not have believed that a stingray could get so big... huge... I was not abducted!

No aliens...

14. Noblesse Oblige

The Islanders of the Torres Strait are a unique people. They are strong, lean, fast, powerful, coordinated, athletic and skilled. Melanesians are tribal people who have sustained a powerful warring, seafaring and permaculture society since before the Vedic Era, if not longer. Powerfully litigious, they know their rights and they are prepared to fight for them if negotiations fail. They fight for keeps, not points. In ancient times they were headhunters.

Today they are happy, friendly, warm hearted people. They love life. Scintillatingly clear minds and spirits from millennia of hunter-gathering, survival and war, they are tuned in, aware and some among them are mythical in stature.

The natural beauty of the Torres Strait is such that one could be forgiven for believing they have been transported to a dream beyond this world. But do not be deceived. It is a dangerous place. It has its laws, its boundaries and its minacious denizens. The realm the islanders live, love, dance and thrive in may as well be another dimension. An almost mythological and intense domain not for the faint hearted.

The navigators of that realm, the islanders of both Eastern and Western Islands love people but they do not suffer fools. Nature's law: 'Get it right or die' predominates here and the people respect it.

Seldom are there second chances when Mother Nature exacts her rule. But there is also a tradition of adopting the homeless. No child is an orphan here. Rearing and teaching young people to be productive communal citizens forms the hub of the social survival structure only slightly dented by the white man's gun and oppression meted out by the colonisers over many years.

There are many stories of adventure and misadventure to be narrated. Stories of peace, love and war. Some will never be told. Many of these stories died with Paul some years ago. Paul was a respected Elder and a powerful peacemaker, though not necessarily a pacifist in the weak sense of the word.

This is one of my favourite stories from the Torres Strait. It refers to the mighty Paul the Elder who is a descendent in the lineage of King Dabad of Erub and the cutting edge of forgiveness. In his early days Paul was a, 'bad' man. Of pure warrior heritage he was not one to be messed with and his reputation preceded him.

As he matured he became a follower of Jesus whom he considered a living example whose guidance he followed. Though he understood well the old Zogo mystical sciences and could easily discern things, understanding also the value of Zazen and other disciplines, having been a pearl diver associating with Japanese and others. The years I was fortunate to know him, he was a seeker and a student of life.

He had worked with many different cultures on pearling luggers from the days of sail and diving helmets, the old dangerous way and learnt much from his associations. His knees still bothered him from the days when Islanders were exploited in deep waters for long hours and some incidents of the bends.

Paul was an awesome fighter and in his bad old days before I knew him, I heard that it finally took more than a dozen men with truncheons to stop him.

Like his ancestors before him he did not play fight, preferring peaceful interaction yet was unstoppable when necessary. He was banned from boxing because he was a quick knockout man even with multiple attackers. The few times that I saw him in action he fought impeccably and he didn't only box. However his greatest exploits shall forever be in the realms of peacemaking and building bridges between people and cultures, healing many wounds to prevent avoidable conflicts and harm.

Paul was a carpenter, builder, fisherman, farmer, friend of the people, a lover and in his own way a sage.

The following happened in 1971, the Centennial year of the celebrated 'Coming of the Light' festival.

Blessed Are The Peacemakers

It was Christmas Eve at Tamwai Town, Thursday Island. People were gathering to feast. Some young men a small distance away began to argue. Then it escalated into a brawl between the leaders of the two major gangs of the region who in those days called themselves, 'The Badu Boys' and 'The Half Castes.'

People noticed and brought it to Paul's attention beseeching him to put a stop to it. They always expected him to resolve altercations because he was good at it. In no great hurry, he casually sauntered toward them.

"Come on boys," he said. "It's Christmas Eve, people are gathering to feast and be happy. We don't want any trouble." In the dark they did not know who it was. Normally with Paul this would have been more than sufficient. His reputation preceded him. "Fuck off, old man. This is our business!" one young thug replied. (Paul was 39 and in his prime) Now Paul never shied from trouble. Instead of leaving he kept walking toward them. Lowering his voice to a warning tone, "If you're going to cause trouble why don't you go somewhere and settle it between you? Somewhere away from the women and children." I think he made an error of judgement and assumed this would be enough but as neither recognised his voice the effect was wasted.

Out of range for a fist or a knife, in a flash in the dark one of them closed the gap by unleashing a belt, swinging it hard. The buckle got Paul in the eye and surprised him. The others from both sides turned on him now. In the flurry they got him to ground and kicked him briefly then suddenly bolted. Had they stayed, even without our backup, knowing Paul he would have got the better of them. Before we could cover the distance, the bastards were gone into the night. They had not knifed him. These were bad men.

Paul was OK. He got up and grunted. An Islander of the old generation it would have taken more than a few kicks to faze him. We put ice on his eye and got on with the feast. For him, the incident was minor and the Christmas celebration proceeded as normal. In the old days he would have sought them out and trounced them. If relatives joined the malefactors he would have come back with staves and friends or whatever it took, until the whole tribe was taught a hard lesson. This was the very necessary old 'payback' method of reparation commonly accepted in the region from the northern Gulf of Carpentaria to Papua, Bougainville and most of Melanesia. In lieu of trade or exchange only war would determine outcomes where there was no satisfaction. Not so long ago, failure to re-establish a clear dominance would mean he would be fair game and his land, assets and womenfolk would be at risk. More attacks would then follow in waves. Kindness would be seen as weakness. But these were different times. The missionaries had brought Jesus and his teachings. (London Missionary Society 1871)

Paul would forgive. Or would he?

We celebrated Christmas but it was not long before informers emerged from the woodwork to provide the names of those who had dishonoured a respected Elder. In the old days, these would be dead men walking and the belief that this was still so was even now strong. So much so that when the culprits realised what they had done, they immediately went underground hiding for their lives.

To Give Back a Life

One day, some months later we were at sea again as usual. That was our profession... fishing! A good life. The competition appeared to be working our waters and it was time to negotiate before a dispute arose.

It was not long before Paul and the captain of the other boat spoke on the radio for a while and decided to meet and discuss sharing and distributing rights to fishing spots for that trip. The Elders cared about the people and it is tradition to seek ways to negotiate disputes first and foremost. That has been the way since time immemorial. Most of the time diplomacy worked best. There were codes of honour to be respected.

Among our crew, the word was already out that the guy who had, 'buckled' Paul in the eye was employed on the other boat. Our crew were convinced that we would see a killing.

There was a murmuring among the crew. Murder on the high seas was not uncommon in the region. Sharks remove all evidence. And the big white pointers were around a lot lately. All variety of fins were surrounding our boat despite the fact that we had not caught any fish yet.

A delegation with Paul leading made their way in an outboard dinghy to the other bigger boat. I was cook at the time, feeding a large crew. Paul instructed me to cook extra because we were going to have guests. The other captain was a friend of Paul, another Elder from the Western Islands.

In the old days before the missionaries, these two groups were traditional enemies but would form alliances if troubles erupted with nearby Papua. Huge wars were fought. Now it was more friendly rivalry.

As was his way, Paul showed his power by visiting the other boat first with only a handful of offsiders. Thereby he also set a precedent and his return invitation could not then be declined without a major insult ensuing that no-one could risk.

By now the crews of both boats were convinced that the fate of 'Buckle' was sealed. Under the circumstances, if their own Elder gave the word they would even do the dark deed themselves and never speak a word of it. 'Accident at sea' would be the official version. No-one wanted Palm Island for life. (An exclusive prison camp for Aboriginals and Islanders.)

This guy had wronged a highly respected Elder and leader of the people and potentially compromised a longstanding truce between two tribes. Anything was now possible.

Time ticked slowly.

I cooked extra for the expected guests as is the custom. The crew began to speculate on the fate of 'Buckle.' They were certain they would witness a major incident.

Eventually two dinghies returned. Ours and theirs. They arrived. I served out the midday meal.

We all ate.

I later heard from the crew who accompanied Paul that he immediately spotted the 'Buckle' who was trying to hide and as they were about to disembark onto the portage dinghy, pointed to him and said, "Bring him too!" They did.

In ancient times in this military culture when two chieftains who were friends made an alliance, such little men as had committed misdemeanours became expendable. To all means and intent, 'Buckle' was now on death row… and he knew it! He was pale with fear, a chilling shade of grey never to be forgotten. The smell of fear which exudes from one upon whom the death sentence has been pronounced is equally as terrible.

'Buckle' did not seem hungry, but he at least tried to make a show of eating. To not eat food offered in the tradition of the region is a supreme insult which could have speeded up the inevitable. The now pallid, 'Buckle' tried not to show his fear by shrinking himself into a corner. He could not hide his involuntary shaking with terror.

"Eat, eat plenty!" Paul welcomed heartily as is the custom. If he was aware of the other man's distress he did not show it. Surely he must have noticed. Everyone else had.

I did not feel too endeared toward, 'Buckle.' He had dishonoured my father and mentor and I was reluctant to offer food to such a one. Paul got in quick with cordial and friendly, "Feed him too, feed him plenty. Feed our guests Evan."

So I did.

In the old customs this could often mean poison. Often to paralyse, so that the victim could witness their own slow execution. It was rumoured that some of these 'customs' were still practised in secret. 'Buckle' knew this and tried to hide his terrified shaking but he could not. It got worse. Nor could he conceal the skin pallor which gave away his terror. I began to feel slightly sorry for him.

Everyone pretended not to notice but you could have cut the mood with a knife. It hung in the air like death. 'Buckle' was too afraid to get up and leave. In any event there was nowhere for him to go. He wanted to vomit with fear but looking downward kept swallowing and forcing himself to eat.

We ate and waited. We waited some more and watched a perfectly good fishing day going down the drain as time passed, missing the opportunity for a great catch. Fish were everywhere! In fact the sharks were feeding in a frenzy all around.

Uncharacteristically, for many long hours the captains planned and negotiated sometimes looking at maps, speaking privately and out of earshot, occasionally glancing our way. It went on and on.. and on… We were bored and wanted to work. Suspicion about the discussion arose among the crew. In their minds it was not a matter of,"if" but when and how.

Perhaps the captains were plotting the disposal of this petty miscreant's body, for he was a known bully when backed up by his gang and had committed criminal misdemeanours. Everyone, even his workmates were now visibly distancing themselves from him.

The crew expected serious punishment to take place. Occasionally someone gesticulated trying not to be too obvious. We found ourselves wondering what it was the two captains were discussing and why it was taking so long. Everyone assumed that it was more than only fishing rights. The tension was becoming more palpable with each long minute.

It was getting colder as the wind rose and we wanted to move and to work, not just sit like this, which was most unusual. We sat and waited. The Elders are not to be questioned.

The water was starting to get choppy and we would miss any chance of a catch for the day. All this waiting and the mounting cold simply added to the tension but of course nobody dared comment, other than to whisper among themselves of, 'Buckle's' impending fate.

'Buckle,' was certain that it was his end and he would soon be meeting his Maker. I think by now he was resigned to die. But not entirely. He still wanted to live. There was no escape in these shark infested waters and we were far out in the Coral Sea outside the Barrier Reef in the great deep blue Pacific Ocean, the Koey region.

Some speculated that his captain had sold 'Buckle' out in order to keep the peace. 'Buckle' was outnumbered a little more than a tad. He simply squatted in a corner, alone, trembling continuously looking like the loneliest man on earth. You could feel the chilling dark clouds and the air reflecting the approaching storm.

After many hours of long, 'island time' covering all manner of hard discussion, negotiations and endless cups of tea, the talks finished.

Finally, slow, dangerous and calm, Paul got up. The other captain got up as well. Whatever they had decided together would be final and accepted between them. These are men of their word. They appeared satisfied.

They would execute their plan.

With a demeanour of dark severity upon their faces they began to slowly walk our way.

"Here it comes" said the eyes of the crew. Some murmured it.

The now isolated, 'Buckle,' sat there with resignation all over him unable to make eye contact, still frozen and looking down. He was a broken man. He had accepted his fate and was almost unconscious with fear in a lather of profuse cold sweat.

The other captain and crew got into their dinghy and were about to cast off to return to their boat.

Buckets of sweat dripping onto the deck, 'Buckle' was sitting in his own wet patch, a picture of unimaginable misery.

Suddenly... Paul moved toward him... Flashing bright white teeth contrasting with his dark skin, Paul smiled warmly, simultaneously detached and compassionate as only a true warrior of ancient traditions can. It was like the sun coming out unexpectedly from behind the darkest storm cloud.

"Aren't you going back? We don't plan to keep you here," he quipped. 'Buckle's' eyes and mouth opened in surprise and he came to life so unexpectedly I think he even surprised himself.

He took the cue and as the others were casting off quickly leaped into the dinghy, almost falling into the shark infested waters trying to hide his fear that Paul might suddenly change his mind.

Had he fallen into the ocean, the gossip would have suggested that it had been deliberate use of the 'warrior's magical powers.' Fortunately for all he did not slip and fall overboard but only just made the dinghy and clambered aboard.

They left.

As darkness fell and the storm persisted, we closed down for the night preparing for tomorrow's work.

Born Again

Months later with a full catch aboard we moored at Thursday Island again.

'Buckle' was on the wharf waiting. He had heard that we were coming and had decided to adopt this Elder.

"Hi, 'uncle' Paul, " he greeted. "Can I help with anything, carry or run an errand?"

With Paul, most things ended in warm friendship, the past put behind and sacrificed to a positive focus of a rewarding future.

From that day on 'Buckle' had become a changed man. He had quit drinking and drugs, given up gangs, even tried to reform the others and quit molesting the island girls as gang boys tend to do.

He had also taken up a course in carpentry, joined a church and was planning to marry showing prospects of becoming a good citizen and never looking back.

'Buckle,' that's not his real name, would often be seen mending the homes of the same grandmothers he used to steal from. He was now a protector. The new year saw a new man emerge. The old one had somehow died.

Paul said nothing more about the incident. The lesson having been learnt in the fullness of spirit the matter was dropped. He preferred to sit around a campfire, joking, telling stories of ancient adventures, making people laugh and cry, remembering times long gone, teaching of ways almost lost. Most of all he loved to see people safe and happy.

Stories tell of the leadership of Barunah, Paul's father, another powerful peacemaker and navigator of sea and souls and each generation of chieftains all the way back to King Dabad himself as well as being the mightiest of warriors, were as magnanimous as King Solomon thereby guaranteeing survival for all in this sometimes terrible domain. This and so much more I witnessed during this most transforming of apprenticeships which I was fortunate to endure, survive and enjoy.

The privilege of association with spiritual giants in a realm of intensity and raw nature has indelibly seared itself upon my soul. They live in the hearts of many and also my own. I lived and dwelt in that unique domain and still do.

To live a life blessed by power and compassion combined and to be able to witness it in action and to learn great things written in living example is worth more than all the books in the world.

To have influence and to use it wisely is a priceless gift!

15. Anchor

As we approached Shark Reef I could see fins of all sizes everywhere swimming in all directions.

This was obviously a meeting place for all kinds of shark, large and small, something like a great convention of sharks of the world, but why the great gathering remains a mystery to me.

It was obvious why it was called 'Shark Reef.' What I saw on the surface was nothing compared to what I was going to see in the water.

Did I write that correctly? What lunatic would go into that water?

Well, the situation arose where there was no choice and it happened like this:

Paul told me to cast the anchor. I did not hear him properly or misunderstood his signal for the correct instant to cast the damn thing and in one of those weird moments, things went awry and the boat swung around in the prevailing current, tangling the anchor rope around the propeller.

Yep! Best place for it to happen… ever!! The only way to bring about the only possible solution is to go in the water and untangle it!

You could say Paul was angry. "What do I do now?" I called out.

"You fucked it, you fix it," he replied. That is the traditional old way of teaching and it is very effective.

"How can I do that?" I replied to an already angry man.

"Get in the water and untangle it!"

"You're joking aren't you?" I replied

"Well if you don't go in," he growled. "I'll throw you in," and he meant it.

Now I must qualify that more than once he had said, "If I say it's safe, it is safe and if I say it's not safe then it's not," but I was hard pressed to believe that this was one of the safe moments. He was very much in tune with this oceanic realm and its denizens, so I would have to run on faith.

With the shark summit going on, notwithstanding that I had already made my measure of sharks at work, it did not seem like a good idea in this instance and I made a good effort to refuse and to argue the point but to no avail. Really there was no other option. It was my mistake and it was my responsibility to provide the solution.

I asked for backup and one of the crew humorously volunteered!

I asked to take spears and the experienced Islanders laughed. They knew that in such places sharks were safe and that it was usually when they surprise you in smaller numbers that you had to worry. That did not register with me, I was the fucking patsy who was going in and having a chat with sharks and fiddling with the propeller. And there were so many!!

I could not have expected what I was to witness when I got into the water. It was crystal clear and I could see for… well if not miles… a damn long way.

The water was so lucid it was as if we were suspended in the air and you could almost see the horizon.

A vast multitude of diverse variety of sharks in all shapes, sizes, breeds, religions, sexual preferences, nations, colours and denominations… cavorting orgiastically.

It looked like millions of them dancing around in all directions as if in a frenzy but not attacking or eating anything… well, just dancing.

The variety was endless.

Some sharks were mildly interested in me, checking me out and swimming away.

I untangled the anchor rope from the prop while the other boy watched my back. That done, we got back onto the boat and cast anchor. This time properly.

Prop untangled all was good!

Over time, I got to know that most sharks are entirely safe, provided of course that I didn't splash too much or was bleeding or had eaten putrefying material and farted. That probably explains why vegetarians seldom get bitten by sharks when they're stuffing around in water that they should not be in.

In those days there were no house refrigerators for the islanders and all food was fresh, not merely chilled, but truly fresh.

In recent years one uneducated person said in a Facebook post, "Sharks are in plague proportions.." and this was somehow supposed to make him and other morons feel good about killing sharks for sport because the dead-brains perceived them as a, "threat" when they invade the ocean smelling bad.

Some people have the fantasy delusion that the shark is somehow wrong to want to eat and that they're entitled to infringe in his domain and keep behaving like dinner. They then blame the shark for doing his job. Such irresponsible arrogance is a sure-fire way to invite trouble.

"Plague proportions"? I've never met a shark on land, ever!! I was rarely threatened by any in the ocean. They mostly mind their business. We all know one species that is in, "plague proportions" threatening all life on the planet, including each other and it ain't the fuckin' sharks!!!

Ecological sciences show that sharks are at risk at the hands of the, 'plague proportion' overbreeding, self important species who are overworking ever so hard to make themselves extinct by killing, pillaging, destroying, plundering everything they can, converting it into 'money' and then racing to see who can die with most toys thereby destroying their own life support system and that of future generations.

The planet will survive. The most recent innovation may not. Humans, whilst the weakest animal have the ability to make tools and technology. This makes our species the potentially most beneficial and at the same time the potentially most able to destroy, including ourselves! Collectively and individually, our choice!

Mind you, when the white pointers gathered even the Islanders got the hell out of the water. They are not to be tangled with. I would follow suit.

Oceanic sharks are simply doing the job for which they were designed or evolved, or both, to keep the ocean clean. Without the garbage collectors we would be deep in it or we would have to clean up our own rubbish or drown in it as an irresponsible species.

What I learnt from sharks in the ocean contributed strongly to helping me survive human predators when they tried their luck, driven by their basal ganglia.

The two legged sharks I was to meet on land were far more insidious, sneaky and dangerous.

Statistics reveal: Three people die from shark attacks on average in Australia each year!!! On the roads, in Australia alone, traffic deaths average over 1200 a year!!! That's 102 each month!!! Before the, .05 alcohol blood level drink-drive law was passed in Australia, it was worse. Globally, all up, 50 to 80 annual deaths by shark, which can be simply prevented by the unskilled staying out of the ocean. World Health Organisation statistics show about 1.3 million traffic deaths annually world wide!! That's one person killed on the roads every 25 seconds. Think about that each time you drive or swim.

16. Warrior Reef

B etween the Coral Sea and the Arafura Sea, between Cape York, Australia and Papua New Guinea is Zenadth Kes... the Torres Strait!

In an area of fifty thousand square metres or so, seventeen of more than two hundred and fifty islands are inhabited.

In 1792 the notorious Captain William Bligh had an encounter with Islanders in the waters near the eighty kilometre long reef connecting Tudu Island at the southern end. Since he was not there to trade, his motives were questioned by the locals. When he refused to communicate appropriately or observe traditional maritime protocols, his ship was attacked.

This reef was subsequently named 'Warrior Reef.' It already had a name.

We had been fishing at Warrior Reef. It had begun with the low tide exposing the reef. We could walk on it at first. The fishing and collecting was good.

All day long we went backwards and forwards from the reef top shuttling to the mother boat in the dinghies, steadily loading up the freezer box. It looked as though by the end of the day we would have a freezer full to the brim and return to Thursday Island and sell this catch in record time.

When you ignore that which must be observed, Mother Nature will kick your arse and teach you humbling lessons. Everything has a price. When you fail to respect the economy of life, the ancient laws of life itself, severe re-education generally takes place. This was to be a day of note.

Towards the end of the day there was an incident where one of the overloaded dinghies had crashed into a coral edge and was leaking badly. The damaged dinghy had sunk and disabled the outboard motor which was now swamped so it could no longer be started.

Beginning emergency procedures the crew from the damaged dinghy alighted to the reef top with the equipment. The dinghy was to be towed back to the mother boat empty and hauled aboard. The catch was transferred to another dinghy and then conveyed to the mother boat while the crew remained behind standing on the reef which was now about knee deep as the tide cycle had begun to rise again.

We had to make arrangements to take some crew back in another dinghy whilst others were stranded on the reef and moving guys from the previously overloaded dinghy back to the boat in shifts was taking up time.

'Time and tide,' as the saying goes... 'waiteth for no man.'

When you miss a tide everything changes. This sudden change had created risk. Emergencies are seldom planned for... 'and all for want of a nail,' so much can be lost but at least some here could draw on their traditional knowledge.

The trouble was this: Several other things had begun to happen at the same time.

The wind came up. The tide changed and was now rising at an alarming rate. To top that it was starting to get dark.

Unexpectedly the wind suddenly stopped and yet the stormy water increased in roughness as conflicting currents clashed. Not a usual event in most places but due to the configuration of reefs in this area it was a regular feature not commonly known. All these things together presented an increased measure of unpredictable risk.

Finally we sent out a boat to get the last of the crew. However if we put everyone from the final trip into the one available dinghy in the now rough water it would have overrun the gunwales and sunk.

Paul volunteered to stay behind on the reef and be picked up in one more trip.

The final group were returned to the mother boat safely which was now a considerable distance away but out there alone, Paul was at risk of being swept away.

The tide was rising fast and the last we saw of him he was waist deep in rising water isolated out on the reef.

The wind had mysteriously stopped entirely, however the contrary tides working against other currents were causing high waves as the water fought itself on and around the reef.

By the time we had every one of the crew back, the water storm had escalated and visibility was almost non-existent because a thick fog had descended. It hung eerily in the rough water, a strange phenomenon common to this area which the Elders understood but this crew were less experienced young men who had not been fully initiated into the mysteries of the region.

The mother boat had now swung around and the anchor had to be drawn or we would have collided with the side of the reef. Because of this we had to run against the tide on almost full throttle in order to keep still while we wondered what to do about Paul who could no longer be seen.

Fighting to maintain control of the situation the crew were at a loss as to what to do. At first, Mark, Paul's brother was panicking. Nightfall was descending and he believed we had lost Paul. The fog was thick.

A silence descended upon the crew despite the cacophony of the storm. Everyone thinking... Paul! What would happen to him? He was the only Elder and our leader and captain. He had the wisdom of the region and we were all relative novices.

For a few minutes which felt like an eternity everyone seemed frozen. Mark at the wheel, was struggling to control the mother boat against the waves and currents. It was not possible to take the boat to where Paul was situated because the reef outcrop was too large in size and we would have been smashed up against it in the altered conditions.

I was atop battening down anything that could move. When I got back into the wheelhouse the crew was standing around looking confused. Someone said, "Who is going to get Paul?"

Silence. No one volunteered.

Conditions outside were challenging and we knew that one mistake would mean we would all get swept away to God-knows-where.

Mark turned the boat into the current again as we peeled our eyes looking for signs of Paul.

Suddenly we saw some flashes in the distance which intermittently lit up the fog ever so briefly creating the spooky effect of a dim but definitive glow that stood out in the middle of that dark violence.

The mysterious ghostly light persisted flashing and then stopped. After a while it repeated then stopped again. What could it possibly be? Some idiot volunteered, "I think Paul has died and that's his ghost." That was the worst thing you could say among superstitious locals. It could cause a mutiny but that was not practical at this time so they all sat there like stunned mullets. Mark threatened to punch the guy's lights out if he did not shut up and stop blithering and I agreed.

By now a form of confused selfish survival paralysis had set in with many of the crew. The rest of us were not about to give up however, not against the tide, not against the storm and most certainly not unmindful of the possibility of failing to rescue Paul in the face of these extreme odds.

But how could we achieve a rescue in these conditions? If somehow that light was indeed Paul, how could it be?

Some fool started to panic and said, "Let's get out of here!" Some among the crew started to debate but this was not time for talk or fear.

I took charge and told Mark to maintain the boat at a steady pace in the deep water for safety. I shouted, "Does anybody want to come with me?" Again no-one volunteered.

At least Mark and I felt certain that in some way the light represented Paul and we would give it our all. For some inexplicable reason Mark usually disliked me but in moments like this we had to work in unison. Despite all efforts it seemed as if we were drifting towards the unknown. The rescue would not be easy if we stopped to overthink it or waited.

Our usual practice was to tow the dinghies behind the mother boat. The last dinghy we had used was still beside the mother boat at risk of getting swamped. Checking that the gauge of a fresh tank showed sufficient fuel, I grabbed it and the rope and pulled the dinghy in hard. Some of the idiots wanted to stop me. I threatened them with death if they even tried it, jumped in and cast off. I threw the empty fuel tank onto the deck of the mother boat and connected the new full tank.

In an act of immense faith, now drifting, I drew the outboard cord to start the engine. Nothing!

It would not start! Travelling in the wrong direction I repeated the starter cord multiple times swearing with angry frustration and also praying hard or something like that, because I don't pray. Not in the conventional sense anyhow.

Eventually the engine did start. Throttling out, skipping over the waves I accelerated towards where I believed that dim light had been.

It had stopped flashing.

I had no alternative than to guess the direction. The only directional guidance was now my innermost... something... I could not understand... but trusted at a very deep level. It happens out at sea... The Great Mystery!

Bouncing around in the waves towards oblivion I briefly wondered whether Paul had already died or what was happening but I stopped myself from thinking and focused on task instead. This was no time for contemplation.

Then again the flash unexpectedly lit up the fog briefly forming a cocoon of soft light which kept disappearing and returning. I redirected towards it. At times when the fog dispersed slightly it became a bright flash. Somehow I knew it was Paul. I didn't know how or why but I knew it was Paul! How he did it I could not imagine.

By now as he later recounted, his feet were off the reef and he had started to drift in the current being taken away. He had been holding position and slowing down drifting by diving down grabbing onto a rock or coral and holding his breath then coming up for air and repeating that with each drift hoping against hope not to run out of reef before we found him.

My God, he had such great faith in life if not in us idiots.

I found him only metres away from the edge and grabbed him. He had run out of rocks to hang onto and was being taken into the deep currents to be swept away!

Hauling him onto the dinghy I accelerated in silence towards where I hoped the mother boat would be.

There was no time for fear. It was done and that's all I knew. The fog was thick and I could not see anything beyond six feet in front of me. Anything in the opposite direction would have to do. I had to guess directionality as there was no visible point of reference to take a bearing.

Then the light of the wheelhouse appeared dimly at first and I steered towards it.

We finally got back to the 'Ina' boat. Nothing was said. Some of the boys hung their head in shame. In silence we throttled out the mother boat's engines to full bore in a diagonal to the prevailing tide, slowly navigating further away from the high risk.

Buffeted and running against conflicting tides I found myself hoping that we had plenty of fuel left in the mother boat. We had expended a lot in this rescue.

None the worse for wear, Paul took charge!

The threat and the risk was not over yet and we travelled for some hours until we got to safer waters.

Sleep is not a consideration when mother nature is storming and in a mysterious way her magical life-giving energy supported us through all this.

A couple of days later while cruising in calm waters towards Thursday Island someone asked Paul how he did it... the flashing light and all that...

He explained coolly that a week ago one of the prospective crayfish buyers had offered him a cigarette. Not being a smoker he had declined. Then for some unknown reason the guy said, "Well, keep my 'Bic' lighter. You may need it sometime.." and handed it to him. Without question Paul took it and put it in the back pocket of the then popular 'Stubby' shorts he was wearing.

Have you seen those stubby shorts? How can anything stay in the back pocket for a week without falling out? But it did. Miraculously.

Of course, in those wet conditions the light would not produce a flame but the flint did produce a flash! Because the air was still and the fog thick, the flash expanded into a glow and illuminated an aura around the ignition point and that is what we had observed!

Can you imagine....? No, I won't even go there. It is as it is and it happened as it happened. All but for a cigarette lighter in the back pocket of a pair of shorts.... a life could have been lost!

Instead it was saved!

Serendipity, contingency thinking and improvisation... and perhaps a bit of something else...

17. The Most Frightening of Sharks

The most frightening of sharks I have ever met was not a white pointer or a hammerhead or any of the big ones but a very small angry black reef shark less than two feet long.

Little, small, petite with attitude and speed.

Why did he frighten me so much? I had something that he wanted, he knew it and he was aggressive about it. Above all, he could move faster than me and this was his home turf.

I did not have the advantage.

Let me explain. I was in the habit of selecting the finest of coral cod and drying them. Out at sea there are no flies to spoil the process. By hanging the fish meat strips on the mast, within a few days it would reach a very desiccated and fine tasting rich consistency. Once dried it would become tangy, saltier and unbelievably tasty. Gastronomical orgasms when grated over freshly fried fish for superlative flavouring!

On this day I had speared the ultimate ideal coral trout. Small, perfect and I knew from experience that it would be tastier than any gone before. This one was going to be of superior quality and ultra special. Better than any, simply perfect and I could not wait to dry it!

Then along came a little shark who wanted my prize.

In no mean terms he let me know that he was going to take it. He did this by first darting angrily and very fast all around me. I had never seen a shark move like this or this fast before. He or she then began towards me as if attacking, then backwards and forwards and returning again, zigzagging at very high speed, closer each time.

At first the reef water was very shallow, only about ankle deep and I thought I could outsmart him.

In the minute or so it took to have this conversation about possession the tide had risen to knee-deep and he knew it. As the water continued to rise both he and I understood that I was the one at risk. Its speed precluded any outcome other than me surrendering the prize or risk getting hurt fighting the little mongrel and I was reluctant to do so.

The little fucker was fast. Very fast!

This recognition really hurt because I didn't want to part with my delicacy but realised that whilst engaging in this brinksmanship the waters had now risen well over the reef and were soon approaching waist deep.

To make things worse my dinghy had swung out of immediate reach and into the open deep blue waters where I would not have stood a chance against this little fellow. One cut from him would have brought others.

That was it!

Reluctantly, very reluctantly and not a little displeased I flung my fish out towards the little bastard. He took it and left triumphantly. I'm sure the little prick was gloating.

I promptly and cautiously traversed the deep blue until I got to the dinghy and left that location.

The tide was up, so no more safe diving was possible for that day.

Besides, in the dinghy I had another cod of not so good quality but good enough. Hungry, I soon found a high enough sandbank unaffected by the tides, gathered some driftwood, made a fire and roasted it.

While enjoying a high protein pescatarian lunch and still feeling the annoyance of loss, I reminisced over the idea of how the dried cod I had forsaken would have tasted had I got to keep it.

Laughing to myself at the vagaries of existence's great mystery, I started the outboard and made my way back home to the mother boat, feeling the bountiful Mother Ocean's beautifully buoyant smile gracefully conveying me without effort.

Once experienced, the scent of the reef is something you will never forget.

The breeze, the salty tang, the vast silent expanse of glistening undulating water and the sun burning my skin.

It was like a dream.

Despite the challenges, life was good.

Moments of bliss like this.... if only everyone could know them!

Happiness and irritation balanced by a greater force!

18. Take One, Plant Ten

We worked in all weather and when I was fortunate to fish with Paul, between us we would easily knock over a full quota before lunch. Then we would either do another round trip or go back to the mother boat to do engine maintenance and other chores, always staying ahead of things. On a boat, being ahead of the game can save your life.

The weather was a friend. In what some would call 'rough,' little squalls, small storms that only last an hour or so, we worked!

Once you are out there, there is no 'time-out' and trying to run from it could get you killed, so we faced it and continued to work or do what was required to stay afloat. Since there was nowhere to hide from it, thunder and lightning meant nothing.

Standing silhouetted and unperturbed against the darkening clouds as he rode the dinghy bow, immutably ferocious as an adamantine guardian deity whilst Nature raged all around, this mythical master of the ocean would navigate the channels of the reef with a slight hand gesture, this way and that and I would steer.

The spray, the wind and rain cut into our skin as we rode those waves and oceanic events. In the beginning all this was different, so very unlike the life that I had known and it was uncomfortable, even painful, as if adapting to another dimension of existence!

However, there was a healing edge to that discomfort. Over time, as I learned to face existence and pay attention to each moment, I learned to absorb the life giving energy of Nature.

I changed, gradually transforming to enjoy the moods of wind, water, sun and thunder. In the early days, at first my mind would play tricks but I soon realised that thoughts of fear were a waste of energy and refused to engage them, instead learning to embrace and tune in to the forces of nature as they took over in the presence of each moment.

It was a mystical experience, a communion no longer separate from life but part of all of that which is Life!

On land we worked ferociously digging, clearing, planting and gathering as Paul had learned from his father before him, old Pop Barunah who had absorbed the wise traditions of conservation survival through the ages, a man who could take down a tree manually to make way for food gardens.

As with the generations before him, his example was The Way. Indomitable in conflict, immutable in the elements and yet in life, especially when counselling grief and sorrow, he would patiently listen with a depth of tolerance viewing through eyes of compassion and spoke with love and joie de vivre. I marvelled at his patience, something that in my fiery youth I did not have.

No words or sometimes few words, the onus was on the learner to notice and glean. When he did speak it had meaning. Paul would often say, when digging yams or other food stock, *"**When you take one, plant ten.** This is the Way, the economy of life, waste nothing! Give back to Nature and Nature will bless you with abundance!"* And he did! Every time he received one of anything he found a way to return multiplied! He paid his way. *"If you don't give back more than you take you will one day come back to nothing! No food..."*

Traditionally, Islanders add real and existing value by not removing value from the great storehouse and supermarket of Great Nature any more than needed to survive or thrive, thereby allowing and assisting recovery. I don't know if he had heard of the words, 'environment' or 'ecology' or 'conservation.' He did not need the words. He lived it daily!

Since you can't eat fantasy, productivity has to be real and food must grow in actuality. Opinions and theories do not grow food or nourish. Where there is no pollution, nature produces in excess and health proliferates as it did before the reef was destroyed.

In most of Melanesia gardens are revered and growing food is akin to sacred ceremony, a consecration of life and abundance treated with great reverence and respect. This type of work is a darn good meditation too. *(Scientists have finally identified some of the Earth's magic such as 'M. vaccae' and other healing fungi and bacteria that live in soil which act like a mind-enhancing substance, easily breathed in and which functions as antidepressants and mood boosters as well as unique mind nourishing substances in the air of forests and other natural spaces. Antidepressant microbes in soil cause cytokine levels to rise which results in the production of increased levels of beneficial serotonin. These augment cognitive ability, lower stress and improve concentration on tasks without the unhealthy side effects that drugs produce. Once destroyed through deforestation, spraying and soil degradation, these are gone forever leaving the world bereft.)*

This way of life may sound strange to people accustomed to going to a supermarket and spending money instead of expending effort, forgetting that it took effort to acquire the money and also to stock the supermarket shelves. If ever you should have the misfortune to be deprived of it, then food will very intensely become your primary concern. When you are directly responsible to nurture that food so that it will proliferate to feed you and your loved ones, you establish a connection with the creative forces of the universe. To take only that which is needed and to give more is the Way that the Ancient Ones lived since time immemorial.

There is no such thing as a weed and herbicides poison the earth and life including that of people. It is of extreme interest that the most healing herbs are most often designated as, "noxious weeds" because they have the qualities of strength, healing and sustainability which they may impart when properly prepared. The older generation of Islanders understood this and many of them were master healers and herbalists, skills they would impart to each generation. I don't know about the people of today but back then I witnessed what people would otherwise call miracles of healing restoration.

A direct descendant of Dabad and the ancient kings of Erub, Paul, my mentor, lived his life in a royal way, from great heights and depths embracing vast spans in his living and his attitudes and yet he was human albeit extraordinary.

Gardening formed the core of this ancient permaculture. Growing food crops. "When you dig one yam you plant ten. That is the Way. Waste nothing!" he would say, smiling like the sun coming out from behind a dark cloud lighting up the world...

He would never engage arguments about religion or politics. Paul would always say, "I don't care what you believe so long as you are true to what you think that you believe and do so with sincerity and fidelity and whatever God is, that greater power then is with you!" He did not like hypocrites, pretending to be something they were not in the name of a god for the sake of impressing others when their actions were well known to be going the opposite direction. His attitude was human toward all people.

Towards life, if it wasn't immediate food it was left alone to live its life and thrive. One day I was diving with Paul. He was a little way from the dinghy and I was closer. Suddenly a huge bunch of striped sea snakes started swimming around. I saw them and made for the dinghy really fast, not quite walking on water but if I could have I would have.

I found myself calling out, "Snake, snake, snake!

Paul ignored me! He was moving slowly, quietly and safely like a dark rock in the water... eventually he looked up and said, "What?"

Finally he swam leisurely to the dinghy, eased himself aboard and again asked, "What?"

He looked down and in disgust said, "Is that all? Pfaff, they're harmless."

"What if they bite you!" I wide-eyedly exclaimed.

"They give you a bit of headache.." he replied getting back into the water. Then he looked back, "With all the fuss you're making you're inviting a fight. Then they'll get you!" he said, swimming through the snakes which parted to let him glide past them.

"I'm not getting in!" I called after him.

"Do what you like!" he replied disappearing under…

'Maybe Islanders get a headache,' I thought, 'But I hate snakes…" I had read that these were deadly and I did not feel sure whether I would survive.. so I stayed in the dinghy.

Paul said nothing. He understood weak people with a kindly heart.

Everything was different here. No books to tell people about the opinions of other people with opinions. Only hard facts, life or death. Cut and dried. They knew what they knew from direct experience… the book of Life and Nature all around!!

Islanders live how they live and children played with the supposedly poisonous Trochus shells and other natural things. Nobody died from it. Over time, I would get stung or bitten by this or that of nature's vaccines... bluebottles and other jellyfish. I've been stung many times. Yep, it hurts a bit. I'm still here!

The young people were a little more intense but the wise older warriors were well partnered and respected their women. Except for the drunks; much like everywhere else, alcohol and substance abuse is always associated with domestic violence. Of course, when the girl had brothers or protectors the DV would not last very long in the islands. That's what I call a good step towards true civilisation.

Understanding the dual wisdom of creation and human nature, Paul would always say, "A man is like an engine without a rudder. A good woman will steer him in straight!" and a bad one, well we won't go there..." and, "Women have unique power different from that of men. We need both or life could not go on... complementary energy magnifies possibility..."

His humour was infectious and his jokes often had a bite to them. Whilst I preferred to work alone, for a brief interlude the crew of my dinghy was myself and Sammy Lakon. Nobody wanted to work with Sammy because he didn't like to work.

Sammy was a kind-hearted old alcoholic and when he could, he chain smoked. The rest of the time he suffered. The driving power behind a drunk that makes him work is that he's working for his addictions, the bottle and often other substances and so he did what he could and then sat and smoked, huddled up shivering in the cold while I worked. Tobacco fucks your lungs for diving. Besides, it is always colder in the wind-chill than in the water!

Only on occasions when I returned with Sammy all the crew would be laughing. When I worked with anyone else no one thought it particularly funny.

After a while I noticed the pattern and kept asking, "What's funny?" and people would walk away or say nothing, often giggling and I knew that the joke was at our expense.

I had to get to the bottom of this.

The picture was this: I would be standing on the bow navigating the dinghy, looking for spots and fish or cray. I was tanned and Sammy dark with his back hunched, his bottom lip drooping with cigarette in mouth sitting in the back of the dinghy, steering the outboard...

Finally after much cajoling, someone told me: "When they see you two arriving, Paul would say, "Here comes Tarzan and his monkey.." .....and each time it would drive the crew to hoots of laughter!

19. Coma

One day I woke up in a bed at Thursday Island Hospital. Some of the crew, my friends, were around the bed.

Smiling, "How are you?"

"I'm O.K! What's going on?" I asked.

"We found you unconscious and brought you to hospital," they replied.

"Well I'm fine now," I said, "When are we leaving? I'm ready." When I tried standing I nearly fainted, my head spun and my body felt weak. I sat down on the bed.

They laughed, "We just got back."

In disbelief I questioned, "From where?!"

"From a fishing trip…"

"Come on guys, stop joking around. Really, when are we leaving? I don't know why I've been here overnight… Let's go…"

They all laughed."You've been here for several weeks, we've been out on a trip and we've returned."

"What? I don't believe you…"

"You were here for weeks. We've been out and back and we unloaded the catch. You've been out cold… in a coma the hospital said… all this time."

"Bullshit!" I volunteered as the doctor arrived and I queried, "What's going on?"

He confirmed the story and the realisation then hit me. Three months earlier I had challenged the sorcerers and said it was all bullshit.

I still think it's bullshit. The doctor said, "We think it may have been coral poisoning, or some kind of poison we cannot understand."

Anyhow I spent another couple of days in bed and then asked to be discharged.

The hospital staff wanted me to stay for a week or at least another couple of days. I was still a bit wonky and had a couple of dizzy spells. That is the reason that I agreed to stay for a few more days. I needed to get myself together because I didn't want to miss another trip.

Ravenous, I got stuck into the hospital food and asked for more. One of the pretty nurses sneaked me some extra food, although she wasn't supposed to.

I was young and healthy with lots of testosterone surging and I knew that I was well because when the pretty nurse bent over to pick up my food tray from the trolley I could see more of her legs and my body wondered what it would be like with her.

Having built up my strength I then insisted on being discharged sooner. The doctor was reluctant but finally assenting with the caution, "It's your responsibility. If anything happens don't hesitate to come back."

In a coma for two months? Was it poisoning? Was it sorcery? Who knows? Who cares? I was given a glimpse of other dimensions.

One thing I noticed very clearly... Time does not exist! It's all the same moment!

Naturally, I joined the next trip and enjoyed a good catch. The past forgotten. Life goes on. The fresh ocean air, all the forces of nature and a day's work were the best medicine.

At night I mostly slept on the deck of the boat. The sea breeze washed over me nourishing my soul. In the day the same oceanic breeze vivified my activity.

Aquatic living, especially when free diving is involved, is spontaneously augmented by natural breathing always expressed from within by first people, without labels. It combines all the yoga breath techniques in accordance with necessity.

When you live in nature and move, meditation, the original conscious state, that of being at oneness with existence, emerges as a natural outcome and the result of life lived and expressed fully, not merely a trend separate from daily activity.

Free diving of necessity combines Kapalabhati Pranayama to charge the 'batteries' for long dives. Of necessity Kumbhaka Pranayama when under the water and so many more attributes, Nadi Shodhana Pranayama on surfacing to clear the nostrils, Ujjayi Pranayama as part of necessity when surface swimming and if you fail to notice your breath, you're dead.

In all its raw power and natural beauty the Original Natural Yoga of Life Itself was fully present here. This was not studio lycra/pretzel yoga, this was dynamic and real and in tune with the universe! The teachings were not verbal but direct and experiential.

I had plenty of practice paying attention to the breath when I had double pneumonia as a six year old so I understood focussing on the breath. I had to in order to stay alive. Early training.

Aquatic life adaptation response transforms. Immersion influences the diver, exposure to the water, breath-holding endurance increases with practice, pressure, temperature changes and all the other factors that vivify and evolves our consciousness. It's another dimension different from land life.

In all aquatic mammals including humans the diving reflex in immersion optimises circulation by preferentially distributing oxygen stores to the heart and brain which allows staying underwater for extended periods of time.

The cardiovascular system displays peripheral vasoconstriction, slowing of the heart rate, redirection of blood to the vital organs to conserve oxygen and the release of red blood cells stored in the spleen which in turn affect the heart rhythm and physiological adaptations to conserve oxygen during submersion and many more biochemical changes such as apnea and bradycardia naturally shared with terrestrial mammals as a neural response.

Exercising these functions augments health and natural attunement. In simple terms magic happens! A special kind of fitness transformation takes place.

Ask any free diver!

20. Daru

Location: Daru Island off the south coast of Papua New Guinea. About 1971. Paul was helping his mates out with recreational beverages they had asked him to collect and deliver.

Sweet Sherry, Dry Sherry and Port. For some strange reason the government of possibly the most alcoholic population in the world, had patronisingly decided that Islanders are not safe to be drinking.

Apparently some guy in a suit slowly being strangled by a too tight tie around his neck, in a drab, square, sterile office somewhere in his abjectly boring life shuffling paper, had determined that the, 'savages' would be driven to violence if they were to drink alcohol.

What he didn't understand in his immense educated ignorance was that they had been making coconut liquors such as Tubâ and smoking the Zoub pipe since the beginning of time and enjoying it for recreational purposes regularly. Very different people, they were no more violent than the whites who had invaded their land more successfully than they could ever invade England.

Paul, always a propagator of happiness and merriment where it was possible was apparently breaking the law at that time, a double standard of a law made by people who are only recent innovations on this planet, he was fulfilling the ancient law of people who have been around much longer.

The law that people who in the face of terrible challenges preferred to be happy at all costs because in this domain each day may well be your last. Cyclones, storms, ocean currents, tsunamis, sharks, sea snakes, jellyfish... sorcery, poison, feudal violence... and sometimes even cannibals!

Under the bunks we stowed a number of cartons of bottles which he would distribute at cost to his friends throughout the region; much to their relief and exhilaration because they were no longer allowed to distill coconut sap. If caught distilling their own recreational beverages they could easily have been sent to the punitive internment camp at Palm Island, an exclusive resort for people with dark coloured skin.

In those days there was no Internet to keep people informed by way of peer to peer communication and it was easy to keep the emerging nation ignorant, divided and controlled where skilled governance was lacking.

We anchored and Paul went visiting coastal kinsmen and relatives as he did wherever he went. He also spent some time with the pretty girl at the store and then came back to the boat. There were a few more calls to be made in the evening and we made for shore again.

A short distance from the jetty we were accosted by a dozen New Guinea highlanders in headdress with spears and they were on some kind of an expedition.

What followed was to give me an idea of what it was about.

The leader of this group began to aggressively address Paul and he was pointing at me. They were talking in local language. I did not understand and I hope that the gist I was getting was not what it was about.

Suddenly the crew of about forty-five odd, began to surround me as if in a protective cocoon and becoming as one united big monster breathing aggression towards these Papuan cannibals.

These were the real traditional cannibals renowned and feared in the region! From the highlands of Papua New Guinea they were tall ugly bastards with things piercing their skin and a bone through the nose. Not the dreaded Kukukuku midgets but worse. Arrogantly confident some held machetes at the ready. Others had spears or a bow with arrows. There were lots of feathers. Bird of Paradise!

They were carrying on in what appeared to be an angry dictatorial way. But you could see that underneath the posturing was not only murderous entitlement but also deep fear. They had evaluated the situation. We outnumbered them and were mostly men from Erub the traditional Sparta of the Torres Strait where for at least 50,000 years if not more, men were bred, initiated and highly trained to be the protectors and defenders of the region.

Both Eastern and Western Torres Strait consisted of an ancient military force who had successfully protected the region from time immemorial.

Paul was quite evidently saying "no" to what appeared to be demands.

Their aggression was in short intermittent bursts which would then recede giving the appearance of a cross between an intense debate and bartering. The group seemed to be negotiating about something. It was not fish. Paul turned around addressing two of the crew, "Go and get a crate of Sherry." They complied and went back to the boat.

No-one would to tell me what the discussion was about. Paul said, "We are going to give them a crate of Sherry instead."

'Instead of what?' I thought. The insistence disturbed me because it suggested something and I wasn't sure what it was, but it worried me!

Some of the crew who had better understanding of the local Pidgin-English were talking among themselves. "We're going to have to kill these bastards…" They were ready for it. You could feel the build up of war energy.

When the two came back with a crate of beverages the senior cannibal took it and then came back and was gesticulating, talking loudly and fast, pointing at me again. "I want the wine and the boy."

Paul said, "No!"

I was learning.

I understood Pidgin well enough to get the drift of what was going on but nuances being outside my frame of reference I could not process the thought but for the disbelief. It was soon confirmed by one of the Islanders from our crew.

Despite the very real threat and the agitation that was going on I did not feel as at risk as I should have. I knew I was safe with the Islanders.

Strong discussions resurged. The cannibals persisted with an air of negotiation about them but the matter was not up for negotiation. Paul ordered the boys to go and fetch another crate. They took off again and came back with a crate of plonk again. It turned out that some of the cannibals could actually speak understandable English. Paul reverted to speaking English so that we could all understand.

Again the obviously senior cannibal did the same performance after taking the offered crate but carried on gesticulating and was, in a primitive way trying to frustratedly make demands. He was visibly agitated.

I refused to believe what I was hearing but I still did not feel unsafe because I had a sense of complete protection from the members of our crew, the Islanders.

As a unit they were standing up for me. I could feel the energy rising and the intensity of aggression as if I was in the centre of the cyclone with a protective shield around me.

Following this insistent repeat performance, Paul again told the two boys to go and get one more box of wine bottles and then he whispered unobtrusively in Meriam Mìr language, unique to the Eastern Islands, "…and bring the gun. Make sure it is loaded and bring a box of cartridges!"

Paul was quite calm about all this but this was a dangerous calm. The calm before the storm and I knew it to be so because he had expanded and his mood became quiet and intense as he does when trouble arises.

The young men dutifully returned with another crate, one boy hiding the gun behind him which he then unobtrusively passed to Paul who was obscured by other crew and grabbed it, stepped out, cocked it and aimed at the head of the cannibal leader speaking strongly.

The headhunters took a few steps backwards and feigned anger. I think it was more surprise. Then the cannibals in unison started shaking their weapons and making threats in what was obviously abusive language. It was a dirty sort of excitement, dark, lascivious and I got the impression they were hungry for blood but were too frightened to draw it.

We outnumbered them and there would have been a slaughter if they presumed to persist in that vein. I was later told, had there been a battle these guys would have been shark food.

Paul spoke quietly but not so quietly that he would not be heard. It was more like a hissing of snake... I have never seen him like this before.

"Leave now! Take all three crates free of charge and leave now or you are all dead.." Words to that effect but in language having deeper and more meaningful connotations. He raised the gun and took serious aim. The first shot was over their heads parting the headdress of the leader. The next would not be.

He lowered the gun slightly. The cannibals bolted swearing abuse.. It was almost comical but for the seriousness of the situation.

When we got back to the boat I asked "What was all that about?" "They wanted to buy you," was the answer. "What for?" I asked? But nobody wanted to tell me. Surely it was not what I imagined it would be.

Eventually one of the Elders explained to me, "White meat is tender and they don't like eating black men because the meat is tough and sour." But there was more he would not tell.

I thought he was joking! Some years later I read it was worse than that. The good news is that eating this forbidden fruit sends the perpetrator the bill and when it does, Prions. Creutzfeldt-Jakob disease gets them. When they least expect it the debt collector comes!

It is the most likely reason that cannibal populations have diminished to hopefully zero. Cannibalism causes Bovine Spongiform Encephalopathy, BSE or mad cow disease. Parts of the cannibal's body go missing as if by antimatter and they bleed black stuff out of their eyes and ears. They get lobotomised from the inside out then decay slowly in immense pain for a long time before, in total collapse, a slow, horrid, painful death takes them in the throes of agony worse than it is possible to describe.

I don't know why such cruel and stupid degenerates exist but nature has made sure that they cease to exist.

Most New Guinea people like anywhere else in the world are good people and they too were predated upon by these freaks. Children go missing.

The stories in some movies such as 'The Time Machine' where in some places, 'Morlock' types exist are not as fictitious as we have been led to believe. Be very careful in your travels and even locally in your suburbs. The highland cannibal tribes are rare and possibly now extinct.

Paul never held the three crates of wine as a debt against me or even thought of it that way. It was as it was. Defence is defence. He did what he had to do to protect his son.

Traditional Islander values had prevailed, integrity and honour. As usual such incidents were forgotten and flushed into the past. To carry such would pose an unbearable psychological burden. We survived and used the skills which were at our disposal at the time to achieve the best outcome. It turned out as it did. The present moment of life being intense we prepared for the next life peak which was coming soon as they always did, as often as by nature as by man.

I'm glad I was there with my friends the Islanders who had always traditionally kicked cannibal arse all the way back to Papua each time they tried to invade the Torres Strait Islands over many thousands of years. But those battles are for another story, some tales already told by Ion Idriess* if you can still find his classical books.

In this instance it was indeed like time travel to a very different domain from that to which I was accustomed, a different atmosphere, a different spirit... It may as well have been a million years ago.

Being city bred and born the implications of that circumstance did not fully dawn on me until many years later when reading filled the gaps.

Survival again had gained ascendancy! A thin thread. Bright guardian angels amid dark hungry demons, I suddenly valued my Islander friends even more!

Before we left we went shopping at the Daru markets. Lots of goodies, food, calicos, fresh coconuts, weskepu, vegetables, a variety of bananas including those you cook and more... We were to eat well on this trip.

I had heard so much about 'Daru Tobacco' and finally at Daru I decided to get some.

Well, what shit! It was really thick, dark, rich tobacco that had apparently been brewed in rum. It came in black twists. You had to chop it up then roll it in a sheet of newspaper.

I was at an age where I would try anything once.

On the boat I chopped it up finely... there's a whole technique to that and to duly rolling it up in newspaper as has become the latter day custom, no doubt for the added toxicity of the ink... That was the modern way, the Ancient Elders used the Jhoob pipe.

I sat on the deck like a king, put my feet up and smoked the one and only foul smelling Daru Tobacco while the boat was travelling towards the fishing spots where we would work. It was strong! The buzz was questionably evil.

On arrival at the work site I did my usual thing preparing to dive and down I went... Like a fucking rock! And I couldn't come up again. Like a fucking rock! I metaphorically shit myself and struggled to surface. Like a fucking rock!

Weak and scared of drowning I had to climb up the anchor rope.

I quit for the day.

So much for being a big tough man and smoking crap. For some time I was not much use.

About a week later my lungs came back and so did my buoyancy. Needless to say I never touched that garbage again. I lost good money on that trip and recovered my coordination by making myself scrub the decks until they had never been cleaner.

Lesson learnt!

21. Sardines

Most sharks are harmless to people.

When I first arrived at Mer (Murray Island), I could see the dark clouds of sardine schools surrounding the shallows obscuring the water near the shore as they moved around. In those early days I had come to believe the usual movie propaganda and in my mind all fins spelled danger.It would not be long before I would learn otherwise. Most Elasmobranchs are relatively innocuous. If you don't bother them they won't bother you. They have a job to do and go about their business keeping the ocean clean. Having said that, there are a few breeds that we should stay away from.

Sharks are a very important species, the idea of which the uninformed find threatening. Humans are doing a lot of harm to the ocean which forms a major part of the life support system of the planet. Our life. Yours and mine. I don't know what they're going to do when that is gone and the oceans clog up with junk and plastic. Few people know this but oceanic plankton produces much more oxygen than trees. From 70 to 80% of the oxygen production on Earth comes from the ocean! Once that ecosystem is damaged humans will disappear and become extinct forever!

I've never known any shark to come onto land and bother anyone but a lot of fools go into the water and bother sharks and other life forms.

Over time I slowly acquired a modicum of common sense coming to this clarity of understanding by way of direct experience.

At Mer because children were swimming near the sardine sharks, in my citified ignorance I was concerned and made some comments.

The Islanders laughed and informed me, "Them fella sardine sharks. All'em no hurtem people. Them fella kaikai sardines. You gotta remember we been living like this for thousands of years, this our home."

It took me a while to wrap my head around it.

Eventually observation allowed me to take it for granted like everybody else that the shark fins around the island were a normal part of life. No child swimming in the shallows was ever taken and over time I relaxed.

At night the bioluminescent plankton glows creating an other-worldly experience. When there is any movement in, on or through the water, the rich plankton soup becomes illuminated and reveals the shape of whatever is moving.

When at night the sharks also did their sudden bursts of speed in order to snack on sardines with their mouth wide open, the water would glow in the shape and form of the shark. The hint of other denizens of the ocean could also be seen when they moved.

By day these huge grazing sharks were as impressive. They didn't bother people and that is why the Islanders referred to them as, "sardine sharks."

It was a symbiotic relationship. In these frenzies the sharks would drive the sardines they missed to shallow water where they could be easily caught by an Islander casting a net. They worked together.

On this trip, in their eagerness to get to land, the crew had taken all the dinghies. The mother boat remained anchored about 70 metres outside in the bay. They left me alone on the boat without any means of getting ashore.

I had a girlfriend named Sabra whom I would enjoy visiting. As usual when the word got around that we were 'in town' she would wait for me at our spot.

That night it got boring on the mother boat alone and there was no special reason for me to be there while everybody else was ashore enjoying themselves. I increasingly became frustrated at the inability to communicate with Sabra who was expecting me as usual.

What was I to do?

There were no mobile phones in those days for me to request someone bring a dinghy, so I decided to simply go. Sliding quietly off the side of the boat, I swam along the bottom to the shore where I met her. She had been waiting for me and wondering why I had been ignoring her.

Now, I was either very intuitive or plain stupid, I cannot recall which or quite simply the sardine sharks were not interested in me and word was true.

It was a non event. At least in the water! Nothing tried to eat me. I was not really surprised!

When we would anchor outside Thursday Island and I was left behind to watch the boat, it was easy for me because I didn't care to get drunk. I would volunteer to stay behind and keep an eye on things and stay away from trouble, as the mother boat had become my home.

Some girls would often swim to the boat and we would spend time together. Grace and Becky and others... One, with a delightful personality decided to be my girlfriend so we started seeing each other when I was in town.

There I was with a line trying to catch fish and nothing was biting. What was the secret? I tried different bait but nothing worked.

One day when she swam to the boat alone she smiled at my clumsy attempts. "You'll starve to death like that," she said giggling, "Let me show you how..."

"That's not how you catch sardines you silly 'colé-man'... I'll catch you some and we can have lunch."

I was carrying on about what bait to use...

"You don't need bait... give me a large hook.."

I gave her a larger of the small hooks. "No, proper big," she said. So I gave her a sizeable hook, which to my bemusement she attached to the end of a thick fishing line.

Dumbly, I said, "That's a very big hook for a sardine how does he get his mouth around it?"

She laughed some more and threw it overboard then tugged sharply. Winding it up there was a sardine snagged on the hook.

Snagging a few more of the largest sardines I had ever seen, totally unlike those puny undersized we get in tins, she then fried them in the most delightful way.

After that we relaxed together.

22. Watcher

Waier and Dauar are Islands adjacent to Mer. That being said, between Mer and these two spooky islets forming the Murray Islands triangle was a stretch of water where the islanders preferred not to dive.

I thought it was mere superstition but I was told there was something big that makes people disappear which lived deep under the water.

When I asked what it was, they said they didn't know and that maybe it was a 'devil,' a generic term for something feared and not understood. Perhaps they were joking.

I did not believe in devils, so one day I decided to go and investigate. In hindsight probably not a wise move!

There I was, reconnoitring and loitering in the waters free diving, exploring, and witnessing an abundance of sea life… I was contemplating whether I should go back and get my spear, when suddenly I felt it!

Something was watching me and if my mental radar served me correctly, it was waiting for me to get close enough so that it could do whatever it wanted to do.

The feeling was unmistakable and very intense! Intense enough to not be imagination. Not necessarily malevolent but possibly hungry or too interested, it gave me the chills but for the life of me I could not see anything looking at me.

There was no doubt that a denizen of the deep was watching me. I had an internal vision of a giant octopus or squid but rather than contemplate or stick around to find out, I took heed and got out of there fast, back to solid land.

Soon we said our farewells and sailed to another fishing trip. I never went to that spot again.

---

23. Spunked

There was no party on my twenty-first birthday. Or was there? I was out at sea and no one knew. But nature did not forget.

Coral made love to me. That was all I got for my birthday! Other than that it was an ordinary working day except that I caught no fish!

I was diving as usual, as we did every day and the lobsters were sparse. Technically this particular breed were called, 'lobsters' but people here were calling them crayfish. Even fish for lunch were elusive, or on this occasion too small. Really, I should have taken a day off and celebrated but out at sea there are no calendars other than the cycles of moon and tide and I pretty much forgot anyway.

Suddenly I was swimming in what I thought was pollution of some kind and it was everywhere. No matter where I went the ocean was full of it. At first I thought I was in some kind of an oil slick but it didn't seem to fit because it was different. Hopefully it was not nuclear fallout! That crossed my mind with trepidation. I was not happy about it.

Wading through lots and lots of sticky, gooey stuff forming out of snowstorms, little starry things that were everywhere, little did I realise it was coral spawning season and I was covered in it.

I had just been blessed! There was a celebration after all!

When I got back to the boat and complained everyone laughed, "It's breeding time for the coral," they said, "It is spawning. Relax, no harm will come of it."

Then it was explained to me how it all works. "At the proper time, at the proper moon cycle and the proper water temperature, colonies of coral reefs all release their tiny eggs and sperm at the same time in an underwater storm where billions of gametes are simultaneously set free into the ocean."

"They rise slowly to the ocean surface, where the process of fertilisation takes place. When the egg and sperm combine and become an embryo they grow into a coral larva called 'planula.' Planulae float in the ocean for days and even weeks before they drop down to the ocean floor again where they attach to the substrate and grow into a new colony. They will grow at about ten centimetres a year forming coral as we know it."

In those days they would grow into a forest of fantastically variegated colours and hues impossible to describe and unless you've been there, another world... and the scent of the reef is like that of a new born baby.

I hear that because of irresponsible waste dumping pollution the reef and all its magic is disappearing.

In those days the reef was a magnificent kaleidoscope of living colour replete with endless varieties of still healthy oceanic life.

There was so much magic down there that you could not believe it. Even the best description will never do it justice. How I wish that I had been able to afford that Nikon underwater camera to capture those irretrievable moments of immense beauty which are now gone.

The living coral has an amazing texture and caresses you as you swim past. Dead coral is calcified and bleached white. It cuts your skin.

Nature does all the life giving magic and fucking idiots waste a life harming all life by contributing pollution and then they die! How sad! All a human being really needs is a roof over their heads, clean air, clean water, quality food, company and the opportunity to improve the quality of their consciousness creatively adding to the greater good but instead…

There's not much else. How much pain and disease and pollution and threat of extinction do we need before we wake up as a species?

Wouldn't it be nice to wake up before you die, instead wasting a life chasing that which can never be caught?

Life is adventure and you cannot buy that with money but by living! By slowing down we can capture the moment. Let the world go by and simply notice and adjust accordingly!

In the old days of 'island time' few died when they waited for the right weather to sail. They either left early well before the storm or simply waited until the danger passed. That's natural wisdom. More recently with people having been plagued with the desire to hurry, too many have unnecessarily died at sea.

In 2020 UNESCO declared the coral reef to be endangered thanks to all the contributors of pollution!!

24. The Angels' Share

Somewhere on the reef. Another day. Up before sunrise. No time to eat. Load the dinghy with spears and gear, fill the fuel tank with petrol siphoned from the drum strapped to the deck, get in, pull the cord of the Johnson outboard, then off I would zoom toward the horizon until the mother-boat disappeared altogether. As usual I would eat later.

We were fishing for reef cray by diving down with a short hand-spear or catching them by hand. Finding a spot I polished my goggles clean, positioned them and dived in.

Alone in the great Pacific I understood why it was named that. It was all peace away from the clutter and bustle of psychological drama and inane circumstances.

Through the day I would make piles of crayfish on the ocean floor. As often happened, sharks soon developed an interest in my catch. Mostly black tip sharks and sometimes white tip ones would begin to congregate and then circle.

When they misbehaved communication came first. I would stick something sharp into them, my spear. Having sharp things of their own, serrated razor teeth, it was the language they understood best. Making my point, literally, they would acknowledge who was boss… for a while at least. Their skin is a combination of sandpaper and Kevlar. Nothing penetrated but annoyed, they got the message and temporarily took off. I didn't like turning my back on them though. They would briefly bide their time and then come back and try again. An annoying game to play.

This day, it was not long before they returned and got stroppier than usual, so I gathered my catch, fired the outboard and relocated to a new spot.

The water was as clear as crystal as it often is in the Torres Strait.

From the stern of the dinghy I could see dark patches in the clear water as I travelled. Normally for safety we would stick to shallow reef before the tide came up. Here it was deeper than usual but I could not resist the temptation to go and check it out.

Over the side… I towed the dinghy with a rope so I could see more clearly. The large flippers made it easier. The patches of reef, rock and seagrass at the bottom looked interesting. It was not long before I found a massive outcrop but it was a few fathoms down.

Descending, suspended as if levitating in the clear blue all around, deeper and deeper I made my way. At about three or four fathoms I found a giant temple-like cavern complex made of rock and coral which appeared to be populated by masses of lobster!

Half way to this structure, temptation presented itself in a school of gigantic moonfish.

Suddenly I got hit by one of those icy cold currents that form channels in deeper water, totally different from the warm tropical surface.

Fumbling with my spear in the sudden temperature change I thought, 'If only I could bag one of these, it would be plenty of food...' My young male ego ignoring the futility of an unprepared attempt and imagining I would be lionised for such a catch, I turned and speared it but did so hurriedly. I missed, got its tail and it swam away with my best spear.

Damn! How I hate hurting things without a clean kill. My favourite spear was now gone. Was this an omen? My intuition suggested so but my intellect knew better of course. I was soon to find out.

Ascending out of the deep blue and into the divine light beams shining down from the shimmering surface, I found air.

Climbing into the dinghy, instead of leaving I grabbed another spear and down I went again. I wanted to visit that cavern.

Locating it, I looked inside.

It was thickly populated with literally thousands of huge crayfish as far as the eye could see. In the translucent, clear water I could not see an end to them.

Bagging these would tip the scales and I would finally be able to afford that expensive underwater camera I wanted to record these magical places with.

Spearing crayfish in deep water was a different proposition. Although these crays were much larger, considerably so, the risk of course was greater and I would have to traverse the clear blue between the bottom and the dinghy.

It would not be practical to pile my catches on the bottom in deep water because sharks would have sufficient time to take them. The time and distance left unattended would be too long to secure my catch.

I was careful to hyperventilate and practice the breathing exercises which would prolong my wind for this special excursion before descending.

This time I made my way inside. Exploring the cavern, the proliferation of huge crayfish looked like it continued forever. The magnificent array tickled my greed. This would take many trips to clean up. I planned to load the dinghy and keep coming back.

This was going to be great!

I decided to spear more than one each dive and bring them to the dinghy straight away.

Back at the mother boat I would pretend it was mere luck and would strive to hide the direction when travelling back out to the spot. We had a week or so left to go. I would be rich. This was a treasure trove that was going to make me good money and I would keep this spot a secret to myself for as long as possible.

But never count your chickens in advance or your crayfish for that matter!

Diving deep was silly because I was exposed but I was young and complements of testosterone; fearless, stupid or both.

Once inside again, excited at this find and in almost disbelief, I decided to reconnoitre and suss out this immense gold mine. Following the ocean floor, this was to be another incident where I failed to notice the incline.

The payload of crays kept going and so did I. It looked as if it would never end and so I kept swimming. So enthralled was I that I had ignored what my internal clock was telling me. I had been under for too long. Still I wanted to see them all and where it would end. But no, my lungs started telling me otherwise more strongly.

Intoxicated of sorts, I had been going deeper and deeper along that ocean floor without quite noticing the gradient.

To make matters worse, the slope inside the cave whilst subtle was more considerable than I had estimated and I had gone in further than it was prudent.

The dive had taken longer than I thought. Whether it was the depth, the descent or the fact that I was feeling euphoric and lost track of time; or a combination of all of these I will never know.

I made my way back to exit the mouth of the cave. It was time to go but it took longer than I had estimated.

Changing my mind I decided to spear two crays in sequence to save a trip before surfacing and hung about near the entrance. Large crays they were. This was awesome… Hurriedly I speared first one and then the other using the same spear with the other one still attached to it.

The second spearing took a few more moments to achieve. I got it square in the centre between the eyes but this delay chewed up more time. It would have normally been an easy catch except that my lungs were now starting to send strong cautionary signals screaming,"SURFACE NOW!!"

Turning upward I left both cray on that spear and held onto it dragging it behind me as I swam. It had been a bad decision to stay under so long but I had taken a chance not knowing if I would find that precise point again.

The tide was rising and the current was speeding up. The worst possible time to go deep as I had been cautioned by the Elders.

The surface did not appear where it should have been. Kicking desperately I realised that the incline had been more considerable than I had estimated and I had stayed under too long.

Where was that fucking surface!?

Years in the water develops amazing adaptation responses where you can progressively stay under longer and longer. It happens when you are working all the time free diving but common sense, wisdom and biofeedback must always be embodied in practice. This had not been one of those times and I had been stymied by a gradient once again… and greed!

Concerned and dipping into my reserves of will and anaerobic stored strength I started kicking still harder for a surface that was not appearing. Not quite panicking but dipping even further into reserves as never before, I was starting to get worried. My lungs were screaming much louder now. I had to release some bubbles of air but the more air I released the less flotation I had.

Not wanting to lose my catch or leave it behind I foolishly towed it on the spear behind me knowing that the cray would remain safely snagged into the barb.

This action both placed me at risk and also helped to save my life because the spear was pointing straight toward anything coming at me from behind. I would not have to reset to aim but simply turn myself.

I did not plan it that way. It was a spontaneous action.

Releasing a few more bubbles, suddenly I felt the presence of something to my rear before its shadow came over me. Maybe it was the movement of water.

Turning, immense jaws were facing me, a circle of large, sharp triangular teeth. The mouth was the size of a door. This was one door I did not relish entering. Less than a metre away and still moving towards me, it was without a doubt after my catch. At that speed the shark could have taken both cray and me in one strike.

Or mortally injured me. I was virtually inside its mouth.

Obviously it could smell the dead leaking cray. For that large mouth I would've been a tasty morsel. There was no time to contemplate.

Spontaneously and with ferocious intent I made towards it aiming my spear already pointing in its direction with the crayfish still on it... at its brain through the open mouth.

I thrust hard and fast!

As I said, having numerous sharp things of their own.. sharks understand sharp! They are also good communicators and understand much more as well. Extremely sensitive creatures... Ampullae of Lorenzini and all that.

At the speed of light or faster it knew exactly what its fate was going to be. I'm not sure whether it was my imagination but its eyes seemed to open wider with what appeared to be comical surprise, then suddenly it turned so fast that its tail almost hit me.

With that force had the tail hit me... Who knows? The wave it made cushioned the potential impact and the energy of the water flow sent me flying several metres. The tail was at least six to eight feet from top to bottom and the shark was big and brown. Very big and long but it had turned on a dime.

In some corner of my mind I was impressed but the rest of me was too busy thanking my lucky stars and determined to get the hell out of there. No ill feelings. I got the impression the shark was benign but simply wanted to eat.

AIR!! Lungs reminded me they were about to explode. Or implode. I had emptied them and was virtually out of possibility and flotation as well. All I had to do was to get to the dinghy before I blacked out or something else got hungry. Or that big fellow returned again! Somehow I did not think he would. We had an understanding!

Would I do it? When you are in such a position speculation is a waste of energy so I simply continued to kick hard and that post-haste.

Only just, I managed to surface and clamber aboard the dinghy where I lay panting desperately...

Had I speared that giant or had he cut me, we would both have been at the mercy of the ocean's hungry ones where the smell of blood carries upstream as well. We both knew it!

I decided to stop fishing and took the rest of the day off sightseeing from the safety of the dinghy, instead checking out the various reef structures and placements, studying the subtleties of oceanic nature…

I returned to the mother boat early that day all but empty handed, without explanation. None was sought.

The guardian of that aquatic temple had spoken and had spared me. I took that message under advisement and never spoke about, looked for, or returned to that spot again considering it to be the 'angels' share.'

25. Hammerhead

It was dark when we emerged from Jardine River mangroves in a dinghy. Having recently come from Bamaga, we decided to go exploring. Some had walked ashore on the low tide but the tide had come up before they could return to walk back. It was now full tide and we retrieved them.

The dinghy was overloaded, eight or more of us all standing. A tad too many. The water was calm when we had gone in. The mother boat was anchored outside in the deep water.

The purpose of the expedition had been to look for wild yams and other land based food sources. Some of the crew got lost and by the time they found their way back overland, the day had gone. We had to leave the collected goods behind for later.

The river was full of crocodiles. It was about four inches between water and the gunwales and standing room only!

You could say that we were slightly encumbered but the water was smooth. If a big swell had come up we would have been swamped and ended up in the water.

Paul was standing push-rowing forwards, softly, softly making our way towards the mother boat. Some of the crew were murmuring and worried but soon we were away from the crocodiles and into safer shark water. Mainly hammerheads.

Friendly sharks the hammerheads.

The younger inexperienced crew were making worried comments and then this single largest of hammerheads I had ever seen began to take an interest in our dinghy.

Ideas about fear tend to attract the wrong kind of interest.

This huge fellow was moving slowly and smoothly around us sensing what was going on. Curious, he was not circling us at first which was a good sign but he looked very suspicious and aware. We were in his territory. We were unusual. He was interested.

Some of the boys started 'ooing' and 'ahhing' and 'what-if-ing.' What-if-ing is a fool's game and it creates danger when none exists or where lesser danger exists.

Last moment 'what-iffing' can magnify risk and make problems happen. Foresight needs to happen well in advance, either from intelligent contingency planning or the fruit of hard experience which can act to trigger immediate, intuitive predictive capability to enable control of a situation. Provided of course, one survives to gain the lesson!

Paul quietly and very sternly said, "Stay calm and don't move; there is nothing we can do now other than continue going forward and there is no risk. If you see me frightened then you'll know that there is something to be frightened about and I'm not frightened. Only don't tip the boat and don't go overboard unless you want to get eaten, stay calm!"

The air was electric.

The large hammerhead was about twenty feet long. That's only seven metres. Perhaps it was larger but I don't want to exaggerate. It was the largest hammerhead shark that I have ever seen alive! It looked like something out of a prehistoric era.

The giant came back once, swam past the other side of our little boat for a considerable distance, turned around and followed us for a bit, passed us and then began doing wide circles around us, slowly closing in... we arrived at the mother boat and ever so gently one at a time disembarked the dinghy and climbed aboard.

Maybe it was not a 'he' but the mother of all hammerheads!

The other hammerheads were not interested and went their way.

Another one bites the dust! So to speak. But only because we followed orders and did not panic.
To panic would signal a death wish!

Mind control. Our own! Nature's creatures understand! Calm means fearless. Agitated invites interest.

When risk is present, it is wise to move slowly unless and until a real need to move fast arises. In this case there was no need. We made it to the boat !

On the following morning's low tide we safely collected the goods we had gathered.

◈

26. The Long Prayer

Anchored outside of Bamaga, Paul, a great recounter of past events told this story over dinner...

In the early days many years ago, one of the older men, when he was younger, fell off a lugger when he got up to piss overboard in the middle of the night and was swept away by strong currents while his shipmates slept.

In the morning they realised he was missing and that he must have been lost at sea as he was nowhere to be seen.

It is said that people go a bit crazy when they're lost at sea and become 'sarupa.' Survival instinct being as it is, he did not let go. He prayed and prayed and prayed and promised God that if He caused him to be saved he would give the rest of his life in His service.

It was a very long time that he was out in the ocean, even after those first days he kept on praying to God to save him and kept promising that he would devote his life to Him.

Somehow perhaps he had found some driftwood to hang on to or he simply expended great endurance and lo-and-behold, indeed whether it was 'The Lord' or his persistence or both, he was finally found by disbelieving rescuers who had long given up and thought him dead.

Thin and emaciated, his skin shrivelled like prunes from extended exposure to salt water the rescuers almost did not recognise who it was.

He had swum or floated for many days and no shark ate him. It appeared that God had kept His side of the bargain and so in his understanding he would keep his promise to 'serve God.'

Among other things his idea of 'serving the Lord' was to go into long detailed prayers.

He became renowned for his hour long or even longer prayers. So much so that some people tended to avoid him because they knew that once he started they would be tied up for a long time while he left nothing out.

It was an expected courtesy for people to stay until a prayer was finished, however the old man tended to prolong his supplications including begging favours for all and sundry which never seemed to end.

The older he got the longer his prayers became!

One day it was the occasion of a large feast. Who could pass up on all that food? A large multitude of people had gathered and somehow this 'aulé' (old man) had either volunteered or been selected to say 'grace.'

As he was praying and the group stood with their heads bowed, a large green turtle slowly came ashore right up alongside the very beach where they were to be feasting.

It is the island tradition to eat green turtle as it's been done for thousands of years. There are no shops such as city people take for granted and the meat is killed for you and wrapped to look appealing. In such places the supermarket is great nature with all the abundance of food that delivers itself your way.

Two young men peeking around, bored with all that waffle, noticed the turtle! Naturally they felt compelled to do something about it and catch this opportunity but out of respect for custom felt bound not to move until the prayer was over. Oh well, the turtle would be around for some time and the old man would eventually stop his rambling.

Gradually the turtle made its way up the beach. Very slowly it dug a hole. Even slower it laid eggs.

Throughout this process the two friends watching this expected the old man to finish praying at any moment but he kept going leaving nothing and no one out of the blessings he sought from God.

Then the old guy began repeating, again! Oh, no!! He either forgot or thought 'The Lord' was hard of hearing and he wanted to make sure…

Delivering the list one by one, name by name, item by item …again… he went on and on and on… giving instructions to God!

The young men now totally distracted and conflicted knew that although turtles take an extraordinarily long time to slowly climb ashore, dig a hole, lay the eggs and make their way back to the water … as they had been watching it… the opportunity would not last forever.

It had been over two hours and the old fella did not show any signs of slowing down with his entreaties to the Divine.

This extremely long prayer was still going… with no foreseeable end in sight!

Having laid its eggs and having buried them slowly over some considerable duration, the turtle was very, very slowly beginning its return back to the ocean.

It would have been so easy to catch. But not for long… even the turtle was making better pace than the devoted old zealot.

The food on the tables had long gotten cold and the young men were becoming anxious with each minute as the tension grew.

Finally one of the guys snapped and exploded letting it rip, "Puk you enné long prayer, banbai kakiai gone walkabout." (….you and your long prayer, the food is getting away..)

And it did. By the time they finished arguing about the length of the obsecration and discussing the vagaries of walking out mid-prayer the turtle had made its way into the ocean and out to freedom.

It put a dampener on the whole thing and soured relations until someone saw the humour and everyone began to laugh.

That day they feasted on cold food. Luckily there were no flies in the islands in those days.

27. Coming of the Light

The now heritage listed 'All Saints Anglican Church' at Erub was established in 1919. It was built below the site of the original London Missionary Society mission house and school using local materials including lime produced from burnt coral, basalt and local limestone. The new Zogo-meta (Holy-house or church) was constructed with the guidance of a local island man named Manai and a South Sea Islander Albert Ware helped him.

The oceanic breeze washes over it and it is a totally different experience from some dusty building at the intersection of a city street surrounded with pollution.

In a sense, I too came from darkness into light. From the bleak and stress of city and into the elemental symphony of nature's harmony and this place made an impact.

What is known in the Torres Strait as 'The Coming of the Light' is a festival celebrated with reverence each year. Paul and his father Barunah who are direct descendants of the great warrior King, Dabad, from time to time would proudly recount how it happened...

~ There had been numerous altercations and invasion attempts where exploiting empire builders sought to expand their acquisitions by imposing here also.

Notwithstanding, the great King Dabad remained sagacious and chose to build bridges between the cultures instead of war.

He had been having dreams that a new era was imminent for the island kingdom and that messengers would come.

In the 1840's the London Missionary Society (LMS) had set out to convert people of the Southwest Pacific to Christianity and it was inevitable that they would arrive on these shores.

On the first of July 1871 from the hill at Erub, Dabad and his men watched these visitors as they approached. Instead of the white sails continuing towards the horizon, they made for the island. The missionaries anchored their vessel, the *'Surprise'* off the shores of Erub in the eastern region of the Torres Strait. (Erub was renamed 'Darnley Island' following colonisation.)

It was heading for dusk when the priests lowered their skiff into the water and set about.

As the Reverend Samuel MacFarlane and Archibald Murray of the London Missionary Society accompanied by South Sea Islander evangelists and mission teachers rowed that little boat towards the water's edge of the beach at Kemus, Dabad knew immediately that this is what his dreams had been telling him about.

Calling his fighting men to follow him down to where the visitors would land, his heart was different from that of the warriors set to kill invaders.

An interesting phenomenon then took place. Dabad asserted his authority and ordered his men to stop.

At first there was dissent. The warriors wanted to slaughter the missionaries who had landed and had kneeled down to pray in the face of peril.

Foolhardy or devout, it worked... but only because Dabad had a plan.

Following an extremely heated debate on those shores of Kemus at Erub, Dabad was successful in convincing the protectors of the island to hold back and let him speak with these men.

To achieve this somewhat unusual feat Dabad had placed himself between the warriors and the visitors and said, "If you kill them you will have to kill me too."

Their respect for him was so great they could not commit such an act.

Despite the differences, Dabad found a way to communicate with the visitors and to welcome them into his home where he accepted the book they offered him although at this stage he could not read what was in it.

There was an unspoken understanding that the values the visitors were bringing were akin to those that already existed and a connection to what they considered to be Divine, the mystical dimensions of Zogo and the commandments of Malo… ~

When a religious invasion occurs it usually decimates the indigenous minds because of a clash of concepts and ideologies but in this case it was embraced inclusively and incorporated over time.

The Zogo-le high initiates were to become the bishops and Elders of this modified way. A new era emerged and although this period of transition was fraught with all sorts of challenges, the core Island values did survive and go on to thrive!

When alive, my genetic father in Melbourne was one of the best tailors in the 50's. He had been trained by Jesuits to be a priest but in the end decided against it. A man of the cloth in two ways. From the abuses of the church that I heard him and mum compare notes about, it was enough to put me off all religion forever. However I became curious and studied the religions of the world as I was growing up. I noticed that at the core of each there was one simple message of respect and the rest was all bullshit and exploitation by crooked middlemen who lied, cheated and mostly harmed the world. All too often they tended to be poor representatives of anything Divine.

But not always! Some are indeed sincere and here at Darnley I found living examples of that sincerity.

After that, all my prejudices had to change. Paul, the man I considered to be my true father, mentor and guide, the one who had adopted me, lived his life in an exemplary way because of what he gleaned from that book and I had to, in all reasonableness, re-evaluate my biases somewhat.

Paul never preached, rarely expounded and I never converted to anything but there was something magnificent going on here that I did not entirely understand. He lived it!

I find all these competing denominations with different interpretations continuing to try and con who they think are pagans and heathens, bizarre and ridiculous!

Original peoples know about spirituality and never needed any help from external imposition. Here they simply embraced the new ideas of the invaders inclusively and with understanding used them to add value upon the foundations that had preexisted from time immemorial. Those of humanity.

As was his way, each day Paul would quietly take a passage from the book and then he lived its highest values!

I never really saw him reading more than once or twice because it was a private endeavour. When he withdrew quietly to open that book you could feel the presence of devotion and power. That sincerity and brightness of spirit was so entirely different to the fakery I had been previously exposed to. It was new and a refreshing view of life.

And then when I got to attend the church at Darnley… Holy shit, what an experience!! Here they didn't merely wail like a bunch of tired banshees in slow motion as I had experienced in the cities but they unleashed pounding it out with traditional drums reaching out and touching a greater power which then came down and reciprocated with an unbelievable intensity I have never experienced before!

It was real.

The women's voices ranging from soprano to contralto and the men mostly baritone and base reaching out into the cosmos! I don't know anything about any 'holy spirit' but I felt like I was on fire and my hair was standing on end. Whatever it was, it was good. A clarity and a freedom previously unknown to me!

It became obvious to me that it's not what you try to take from a square building made of brick and stone but what a gathering of sincere people united as one, bring to it.

Authenticity of purpose, powerful values…. the quality of consciousness and the offering of good intention multiplies exponentially and shines in a mysterious and powerful way!

Seeing people striving to live dynamically with integrity, so much more powerful than the sad and insecure begging for some sort of salvation one often sees in those who cannot see the untapped completeness already existing within themselves, can be refreshing!

I still hold no beliefs but I experienced what I experienced and it left an indelible mark upon my soul! A good one. As with a thunderstorm where there is no hypocrisy when lightning strikes purely and without bias, this clarity of awareness and intent I often found here.

Cemetery

Many people do silly things for a dare! When I heard the crew talking about the dangers of walking through an Islander cemetery at night alone, I quietly dared myself to determine otherwise.

'I have nothing to prove' I told myself but deep down I knew that too much proving can sometimes bring calamity and it was with trepidation that I took those steps.

At the nearest opportunity at T.I. I did it. I took courage and made my move. Youthful ego, eh?

On a full moon I went into the cemetery, walked through it and stood in the middle.

And then I felt it!

It was a very intense experience such as nothing I had known before. Not like that of the fiery magnificence I had experienced at the church at Darnley but a cold and clammy hungry sort of chill trickling up and down my spine!

Not evil but not necessarily benign either.

My hair stood on end and it was as if many presences were behind me and all around following and watching.

I distinctly felt like I was trespassing and did not stay there long, partly out of respect, partly out of the fact that I felt like not only was I being watched but that if I stayed there any longer I could have been made even more uncomfortable in a way that I did not want to find out.

Recalling stories I had heard of the Lamar and Nilar Makrem... of ghosts and interdimensional beings... I tiptoed quietly away.

I never tried that again.

28. Weather

Weather often forms the subject of inane small talk. In some realms however it is considered to be life itself!

People unhappy with themselves often whine idly about the weather always contrary to that which is, as it is right now! They dump their own conflicted thinking, unhappy thoughts and attitudes onto the weather revealing how they choose to respond to Nature by filling the airwaves with noise.

Whether we agree with the weather or not, weather keeps us alive and exercises our adaptation responses with a living variety of nuances and sometime moderate extremes to give life.

In order to live fully, it is best to be in relationship with the forces of Nature that go into our making. After all, we can at least acknowledge that we are intimately connected to air, water and minerals.

If we don't breathe, we die. If we don't hydrate we die. If we fail to eat for too long or eat too much too often we place our health at risk. Extremes of temperature can kill. We are fragile creatures.

The weather is ecologically interactive to us, not only immediately but also long term depending on how we pollute the planet or otherwise. So whingeing about the weather is not very intelligent. I suppose if you're a dedicated whiner and you have nothing else to whinge about, the weather may not strike back.

But can we be sure of that?

In recent years some claim we have affected the climate and the effects are now coming home to roost.

Somebody once said, *"Everyone talks about the weather but nobody does anything about it."*

These fellows did! Perhaps it is time that we started to do something about it too, but with a responsible long term view in sight.

One day this happened: A handful of New Guinea men sailed down to Darnley Island to trade.

I forget what they were after. They were considerably different from the Islanders and some of the Islanders viewed them with suspicion.

In ancient times they had been traditional enemies with some tribes. However for trade there were always allowances made and in these times trade was the way to go.

So they did business.

The Islanders gossiped behind their back saying, "They're not very smart; they have sailed down but the wind would not be changing until the Sager season several months later…"

They had sailed down on the Naigai, the Northerly winds which blow from October until December.

As far as the Islanders were concerned they would have some trouble getting back to New Guinea any time soon in their primitive sailing canoes without an engine and they could certainly not row fast enough against the strong prevailing winds and tides.

They would have to wait until the Sager season when the South-East Tradewinds which blow from May to take them back; and the Islanders did not want to accommodate them for that amount of time.

There were grumblings and complaints in case they tried to ingratiate themselves. Mischievous supposition of course.

Somebody suggested the possibility of them becoming stranded but the New Guinea Elder said, "No problem!"

Some of the Islanders still sniggered behind their backs and continued to gossip about how silly they were.

The day before it came time to depart with their canoes full of provisions and victuals they asked to speak with a local man some say had been a sorcerer. Doing some kind of a deal with him they requested certain items and a couple of chickens.

The local, 'sorcerer' appeared to understand but the rest of us didn't have a clue what was going on.

Perhaps some of the older Islanders did know but would not speak of it.

All night long the New Guinea men sat on the beach adjacent to some rocks and carried out a little ceremony where they sacrificed the chickens, chanted and did other things which we were not allowed to witness.

The Islanders, at least the older generations were said to have the Zogo and sorcery and the New Guinea people have something similar yet different not entirely understood by the locals.

In the morning when they were saying their farewells, the oldest of these fellows raised his hand towards the sea chanting some kind of a mantra and threw some items into the ocean.

And this is where it gets interesting.

Gradually a wind came up in the first direction they wanted to go which seemed anomalous. It didn't look like they would get home going that way.

"Silly plan," some said. "they are going to get lost going that way....

They sailed out beyond a certain point and while the locals were still sniggering the wind suddenly changed again at the precise spot to take them around the reef and directly to New Guinea.

We watched until they disappeared over the horizon and wondered.

After the arrival of the London Missionary Society (LMS) and the banning of traditional cultural practices, such things were not seen as often in the Torres Strait.

29. Xmas Not Arrived

Someone recounted this to me. In order to protect the guilty, he and the girl shall remain unnamed.

It was Christmas Eve at Darnley. The culprits met on a tryst at one of the villages which was deserted because everyone was at the church praying. It was not long before they agreed to have sex and found a suitable spot.

Soon they were going at it but in the middle of it all, their conclusion of the village being deserted was soon proven wrong.

As it happened, the old man with the gammy leg did not feel like the long walk to the church and had stayed behind. In a pious mood and not wanting to be left out of the celebrations he decided to put some Christmas music on his old record player. It was one of the really old ones, with a horn, that you cranked or wound up by hand, a vintage His Masters Voice (HMV) gramophone from about the 1920s or 40s.

The LP got stuck on a groove and a Christmas hymn kept repeating, "Come oh ye faithful..." "Come oh ye faithful...come ye oh come ye.." "Come oh ye faithful..." "Come oh ye faithful...come ye, oh come ye.."over and over and over and over and over again.

Presumably, the old fella had gone wandering off somewhere probably digging in the garden because it continued non-stop.

Well, being so instructed made it difficult to perform and the lovers couldn't finish!! Instead they burst out laughing until tears came from their eyes.

The irony was outstanding. They did not consummate.

As for fidelity… well it does not appear there was any of that present either.

30. Nailed It!

There was a sweet old lady at Darnley Island who was suffering from hypothyroidism. She kept growing and she became so huge that she died from complications.

We heard and were called to participate in the funeral. While we were trying to take a rushed shortcut through the reef, the tide beat us and the propeller got caught.

At high revs the sudden impact caused the drive shaft to shear the gear teeth and there was no longer any grip. The universal joint coupling could no longer transmit power from the big diesel engine to the propeller shaft.

As in life, drifting is not a good proposition and as often happens when these situations occur, we were drifting towards danger. As I recall, it was serious danger having no control of the mother boat, the trawler, MV 'Ina.'

So we towed her with a dinghy for the time being. That works surprisingly well but would not be practical for the long haul. If currents became stronger or a bad storm came up it would not have been good. As it was, the existing tide was posing an almost unnoticeable challenge quietly pulling us out... and out... further from the intended destination. Most often the danger was that of getting drawn into the great barrier and the dangerous water interaction there.

Paul got into the engine room and I assisted dismantling some components to ascertain the problem. He contemplated briefly... then he said. "Get me that box of big nails." We had some left over building material, bits and pieces stored in the bunkhouse.

I did. He then set about packing the driveshaft firmly where the broken gear teeth would have been, connecting the nails so that the shaft would gain the purchase needed. It was hard work in that cramped compartment but in about thirty minutes it was done and ready for testing.

Meanwhile we were drifting despite the efforts of the two dinghies now towing.

We started the engine and the repair held. Testing under acceleration it still held and dropping the revs to a moderate cruising speed we headed away from danger.

In the course of time we would go to Thursday Island to order parts and book in with a marine mechanic to engineer it back to specifications.

The parts would take quite a few weeks to arrive. It was close to the day of the funeral and we could not wait. Since the nails were holding so well, we went straight to Darnley instead.

It took twenty pallbearers to raise the coffin and to carry it up the hill to the cemetery at Darnley. We had to make a scaffolding out of large bamboo so that more men could participate in the carry. The old dear must have weighed a ton. These were strong men but we struggled.

Of one mind we pitted our power against that steep incline of the Darnley hill and made it to the sacred ground. I was one of the pallbearers and through it all it felt as though I had all the weight on me but that was only because I was not very strong in comparison to the others.

It was a team effort and we succeeded!

This blessed soul got the dignified burial she deserved. We then made our way back to T.I. and the protracted wait for the engine parts to arrive before we could travel to work again.

That long wait holds many stories to be told another time.

31. Glassed

It was not until I got to Sydney that I had heard the term 'glassed.' Glassing is where somebody breaks a glass object in order to create a jagged edge then attacks you with it. Maybe I simply hadn't been paying attention but it was only recently when I had time to focus on these recollections that I realised that I also had been 'glassed.' Well almost…

This is how it happened… I first need to precede with what brought it about. Being in my early twenties with all the fun around me, Paul noticed I was alone and introduced me to his cousin Rosabelle, a lovely lady twice my age.

We started seeing each other and it was a good relationship.

There is a custom in the islands similar to many cultures where relations out of marriage are frowned upon. Spontaneous love matches are prolific but as happens world wide, relatives mostly won't keep their nose out of lovers' business and are usually unhappy about choices. Especially if they ain't getting any themselves!

Little did I know that Rosabelle had a brother. I never asked, she never told me. I found out the hard way…

I was walking aimlessly exploring the path at Darnley Island, wondering how far it went and what was at the other end. Paul, my adopted father, the owner of the boat we were working from, was in a council meeting with Elders and I was bored.

So I took off alone on the path that goes around the Island.

Somewhere between the villages I saw a guy standing there with a bottle in his hand swaying slightly. My instincts told me to be on guard but I relaxed because it being home Island how could there possibly be trouble?

Well it was not really trouble... but very intense communication... at first.

Sebasio, Rosabelle's brother, had been waiting for me. I soon found this out because he introduced himself. Then it began, "You know our customs... if you can't block the brother's hand, you can't touch the women!"

It was a good custom designed to protect ladies from abuse from menfolk of bad intentions. Sometimes it backfired as in this case and many other happy relationships that emerged by mutual consent were often harmed by angry relatives who misconstrued good intentions.

At first the young man was threatening and then he changed and became amenable and even voiced his approval of the relationship.... After some time a dark countenance beset his demeanour... "Have a drink! he said.

Anywhere in the world this always spells trouble of some kind or another. Whether it's a brawl or some kind of seduction or theft, it never bodes well when someone attempts to numb your mind by plying you with substances.

"I don't drink," I replied respectfully, "But thank you anyway." By refusing to accept food or in this case drink, I was treading close to the edge of another entrenched and ancient Melanesian custom.

This day was to confirm a vital lesson and the lessons gleaned from this incident would save my life in future ones, in particular one of the most egregious of possibilities. I have to thank Sebasio for bringing the lesson. (See *Book 2 - 'New South Wales CLOSE SHAVES', 'Black Metal Gun.'*)

"Well, if you're not gonna have a drink, then come back to my place and we can talk.."

"I was about to head back..." I said, "I think they're waiting for me."

He evinced an enraged countenance and leaning forward with the irrational logic of a drunk he shouted, "Bullshit, you can't fucken' bullshit me! Come with me or else you'll have to fight me here and now!"

"No, I don't want to fight you, I've got nothing against you, Sebasio..."

"But I've got something against you, stand up and fight, fight me now and you can have my sister if you block my hand..."

"Not interested. She's made her own decision and we are both old enough to do as we please," I replied.

"Then fight!" he replied, putting the bottle on the ground and shaping up unsteadily.

It would not have been a fight, poor fellow. But he did not seem to realise it and I certainly had no desire to give him a hiding.

Knowing what I know now, perhaps I should have, because in doing what I was going to do next, this then became the point of capture, a serious consideration in pre-incident indicators.

I could have at least put up a show and taken a few punches to make him … well… less perturbed or something like that but the possibility did not occur to me at the time.

"I refuse to fight you," I said.

"Come on be a man, fight!" He started swinging and punching… I pushed him away, deflected, moved out of the way; he kept going and I kept refusing to fight him. Inebriated, he soon got tired.

Out of the blue he smiled and said, "I like you Evan, come back to my place and I'll cook up some food."

The charm of the devil! I could smell it.

I decided to appease him anyway and we began to walk back toward the village of.. It was near where Green Hill is now and a long march.

We walked for a considerable time and finally arrived at his isolated little house on the hill overlooking a cliff near the ocean.

We sat at his table. He cracked another bottle, poured two drinks and slid a glass defiantly towards me. Of course by now I knew what this meant. A refusal could mean trouble.

He started rambling and talking about all sorts of things trying to achieve a distraction but my focus became more intense. I could feel the impending escalation. His intention was different to his mouth noise.

I knew now that this was a trap and that I had walked into it. I had no fully conscious idea of pre-incident indicators back then, rather noticing the obvious, intuitive 'feelings' and making split second decisions. My folly and my knack was that I liked to explore possibilities and outcomes. This was a gift of learning.

Each time he turned around I turfed the drink out the window pretending to sip as we went along. I had to do it at high speed capturing each moment.

He kept pouring and I kept throwing it out whenever I could, all the while faking sipping it when he was watching.

I was fanatically abstemious in those days. Because of my athletic training I had come to realise that putting toxic shit into your system can make a great difference, a whole second of difference and that can either win or lose the race or such as in this case, determine the outcome of a survival situation.

Coordination and clarity of consciousness makes the difference!

Suddenly, without warning he broke the bottle on the edge of the table and without a pause thrust it at my jugular. I deflected it with my left hand and simultaneously punched him hard directly on his left cheek bone with my right, trying to do as little harm as possible.

I had nothing against this guy. He was not an enemy. Merely an angry brother, intoxicated off his skull trying to clumsily fulfil an ancient custom that had good purpose although he had misconstrued the situation somewhat. I put the extreme misbehaviour down to whatever it was he was under the influence of.

I chastised him and then picked him up, helped him to sit down, telling him what a silly action that had been.

Then the previous debacle repeated; pour drink, pretend to drink, out the window and so on…

This continued for a while and then suddenly again almost identically, when the new bottle was almost empty he broke it and lunged at my face with it.

In an almost photocopy of the previous instance, I deflected and punched. Yet again he fell back but this time on the broken glass that he had caused in the previous instance.

The sharp cutting made him leap up fast in pain.

This time I yelled louder than before. I needed to frighten some sense into this fool.

I chased him, acting enraged but keeping it safe.

Although the protective fire had now come up in me, it was not destructive but I let it rip vocally and postured strongly. I needed to make my point before this sad and lonely fellow did some serious harm to either himself or me. I also needed to get away from here safely for both our sakes.

To get the message across I allowed myself to escalate vocally. It worked. He ran. I chased. He tripped and fell and tore himself up on the protruding rocks of the path outside his house.

He sprang up again ran and tripped again falling forward and tearing himself up yet again. I cringed. I could feel his pain.

He ran and hid. I decided to go home.

Suddenly, behind me there he was approaching again this time playing a guitar and appearing to be serenading. As he got close he turned the guitar around to swing it at me by the handle so I took it off him and broke it over his head. I felt sorry for both the guitar and him. It was an act of vandalism, a spontaneous reaction on the spur of the moment.

I yelled, "Stop this nonsense!!"

He took off again.

Again I started walking back towards the main island. I was sad for Sebasio, I felt sure that sober he was a nice fellow.

I could hear him screaming and his rushed footsteps running behind me. I turned. This time he had a long spear in his hand positioned to strike.

'Oh no!'I thought, 'He's going to end up in jail if he kills me, otherwise I'm going end up in dire straits because he's got lots of relatives here.'

I ran towards him and as he thrust I performed a Taisabaki action and took the spear from him. Flogging him on the back of the legs with the bamboo, he ran again and I after him.

I was worried because the nearby cliff edge was close and it was a fair way down to those huge rocks. There would be an injury or worse if this escalated any further.

Then out of nowhere there appeared three island policemen. Two grabbed me and hauled me to a nearby hut where one sat on me and the other one took off to help his brother-in-arms to, 'arrest' Sebasio. Apparently he was always doing variables of this kind of shit when he got drunk.

I was glad they were putting a stop to it and lay there thanking the gods for the intervention but what I could hear going on outside sounded really cruel. They were pummelling the hell out of him. It was a 'measured response' in their view. Perhaps they knew something I didn't and he had been a bad ambassador.

One policeman came back and asked me if I was okay and then escorted me back towards Dadamud village the way I had come from.

Paul didn't want to hear about it. Somehow he knew. "Don't talk. I don't want to know. Go back to the boat." I did. It was never spoken of after that.

Some weeks later I had cause to feel deeply sorry for Sebasio again.

It was a wedding and there was Sebasio, black and blue and swollen, perfectly decked out in the neatest suit and he was preaching the gospel and 'bearing witness to his sins and of salvation' "…..I once was lost but now I'm found.. The holy spirt has touched me….The bottle once controlled me but now I've cast out the demon drink…

and I caution all you young people to never go near the grog.." He continued quite eloquently in a religious sort of way although somewhat inappropriately for a wedding.

Somehow he had, 'repented' and become 'saved' joining the, 'World Church,' one of the recent denominations that was fishing for souls in the region.

As far as I know he never drank again and I thought to myself, "What a strange way to bring about a transformation.." but then again it is said: 'The Lord works in mysterious ways!'

Some kick-arse 'Lord' that one!

32. Grouper

We had finished a situation where immensely huge white pointers had tried to take a chunk out of the side of the mother boat, the MV 'Ina' when we were cleaning fish.

They had gotten too excited when the offal we were disposing overboard had acted as berley and they tried to chew the side of the boat off.

The sons of bitches were gigantic. Although the reality is different to silly movies, this was indeed of concern because they brought their mates and so as required by the laws of nature, we had to shoot one or two to send them a message.

Their mates ate them and then left and we left that position in the ocean as a marker.

The boat still has the tooth imprints.

We moved to another reef spot in an entirely different area. When changing spots like this, travelling in deep water, we would tow a line with a shiny new kitchen spoon or whatever we could improvise as a 'spinner.'

Invariably a large Mackerel or a Tuna would bite the bright flashing thing that looked like a distressed small fish and would get hooked thereby.

We would haul it in. Mackerel have white meat and tuna deep red. Filleting them immediately, we cut the meat into pieces about the size of a thumb and then marinated the cuts in a large bucket or a bin in either lemon juice or vinegar. Dipping the fresh cubes in shoyu, we would then enjoy them raw.

The original fishermen's Sashimi. You could feel the power coursing through your body. Awesome bodybuilding energy food!! The raw meat of these large fish would feed the crew... twice! What was left was cooked for the evening meal.

When we arrived at the proposed new spot, Paul decided to go and study it. He'd had a strange feeling about it. Not having seen it or been here before, he told us to pause for a while.

He went down and did some reconnoitring. He was under a bit longer than expected. Considerably longer than usual. We began to get concerned.

When he came up he was very intense. He had gone down without a spear, a giant groper had tried to vacuum him into its mouth and it was a bit of a job climbing out against that indraft.

He surfaced, found a short thin spear, briefly mentioned the incident and went back in and was under for another duration of time until we were concerned that the damn thing had eaten him.

Then a four gallon drum floated to the surface with an immense stink along with a huge grease slick and stomach contents comprising all sorts of partly digested items.

Still Paul was not up.

We were getting seriously worried, half expecting an arm or a leg or human body parts to surface.

As some of us were starting to prepare to go down and see what was going on, up floated a fat grouper the size of a goddamn limo.

I've never seen a coral trout that big!!!

Not long after, Paul came up and said, "Okay it will be safe to dive here now," and we got on with the day's work.

Some leaders lead by leading!

Islanders have a system and order that works impeccably to maintain the balance of the nature of the region. They take what is needed and no more. With the advent of industry that changed considerably. In those days large foreign super trawlers were poaching in Australian sovereign waters and fishing out our stocks and our government was doing nothing about it.

33. There Were Giants

//

I'm not allowed on my own land," remonstrated Eddie. "We have our laws, 'Malo Ra Gelar' but nobody takes notice. What kind of world is this?" He was suffering and as he usually did, spoke about the loss of his land and the injustice of it having been taken away. He was very intense about it and always captured the attention of those who heard him.

We were sitting in the wheelhouse of the boat, the MV 'Ina,' anchored outside of the Old Lockhart River Mission. Eddie was so upset that he could not eat. A major discussion was taking place which in my youthful ignorance I could not have known the historical importance of, either past or in the future to come. I was relatively new to all this but the Islanders had been enduring it all their lives.

I had always liked Eddie. Something about his demeanour reminded me of a rock star. In my mind's eye I would always see him on the stage with a guitar and thousands of people cheering his songs. But then again I had a vivid imagination.

On many occasions he would meet with Paul, his cousin. They would have long discussions. Eddie was a man on fire, a man with a purpose, a man determined to win back what was his and to me he was a cool dude even though back then I did not really understand what all the intensity was about.

On this occasion Eddie had temporarily joined the crew, not to catch cray but to travel and confide with Paul. He was on a mission. There was more to Eddie than met the eye. Like Paul, despite the odds of that era he was an educator and an ambassador for Torres Strait Islanders. He also worked hard to heal rifts and to build bridges between cultures. These were men of stature.

The discussion was among the Elders but not knowing any better in those days I interjected with the naïve simplicity of a child, "Learn the white man's law. Learn it well. Use it. Reveal your ancient laws to the world... their laws have only been around for a little time but yours span the ages.. there must be some value in finding a commonality of justice principles. Especially the part about not trespassing on another man's land and not stealing... that's pretty much universal and even Moses reinforced that one!" I then went back to daydreaming and boiling the billy to make more tea.

Eddie wanted to see his home Island of Mer and his heart was aching for it. I could understand.

Perhaps he did not yet realise it but Eddie Koiki Mabo had already begun his victory march. It would be a very long and arduous journey and he would not see success until six months after his death in 1992.

We all now know that he left a legacy for the world!

The Islanders were still being oppressed in so many ways back then. The Australian version of apartheid, the White Australia Policy was still in place at that time. Among other things Torres Strait Islanders and Aboriginals had been banned from alcoholic beverages notwithstanding the fact that they traditionally produced their own recreational beverage named Tubâ usually from coconut sap. They also smoked the Jhoob pipe and grew their own tobacco.

Islanders had known natural freedom from the time immemorial, long before the marketing of the idea was brought to the beneficiaries of unpaid labour by the same marauders who subjugated whom they could capture into secret slavery. The history of 'blackbirders' kidnapping islanders against their will to work as indentured slaves in the sugar cane fields of Queensland is well known. The so called 'Kanaka' had identity in their own land before being forcibly dispossessed.

Little did I then know that this immensely abundant tropical paradise had been relegated the title of, 'nullius' by those who had striven to bring their own moral desert to this rich and noble land.

The bringers of nullius temporarily lorded over, knowing full well that the opposite of nullius was true. For over two-hundred years they plundered the mass abundance and resources striving hard to turn this immensity into a nullius by irreversibly consuming more than needed.

Right now the whole planet is at risk of being made into a 'nullius' desert by the same corrupt values which have infected the morality of humanity.

'Terra Nullius' was the cover story to hide the plunder that was taking place. But as they do, in the end, empire builders fail. They keep trying and they keep dying as great Nature invariably eats their bones again and again and still they learn nothing.

We do not come to life to destroy but to create and Nature is a bitch. She exacts revenge and always takes back what is Hers. It was all a loan. Did we use it well?

'Malo Ra Gelar,' the respecting of the property of others does not seem to enter the purview of those desperate to acquire too much more than they will ever need before they die. In those 200 years of piracy and pollution, the pillagers finally appear to be succeeding to bring their own bereftness.

Greed and stupidity has killed the magnificence that once was The Great Coral Reef. I never would have believed it but perhaps 'nullius' is a possibility after all. The smarter ones are travelling to Mars and going to find themselves a plot of desert there instead of desertifying the beautiful blue planet. Perhaps they will perish there but at least their plan has more integrity.

In more recent times at least, a portion of the global population have come to realise that extractive economies have led to environmental degradation. Despite the fables of the deniers, when the air we breathe is polluted through the reduction of trees and the oceanic ecologies already reduced by 40% or more, when the earth is contaminated and toxic and can no longer grow food, when the waters have been poisoned to a point where we can no longer safely drink and it all reaches saturation point, when the life support systems of insects and worms and all that sustains The Tree of Life die out, Nature will judge us all and let me say this; She will do so without mercy and with finality and evict the poor guests that we as a species have been.

Unlike the global flood of previous ages, it will not be so sudden that we will not have sufficient time to reflect and gain clarity about the reason for our mass destruction and realise that it was we who did it, whether actively or by allowing the abuse of life.

Back to Lockhart, these were thought to be modern times and we were helping out his kinfolk by delivering uncommon articles and material on the way through our fishing journeys. Here at the old Lockhart River mission I could not understand why such great beauty and abundance had been deserted.

I was soon find to out.

We found an idyllic town complete with a cathedral made out of paper bark and gumtrees, the Church of St James which was built in six days. Nobody teamworks as well as islanders!

The most amazing floral array surrounding beautiful little houses that had been hand-made by a united nations of Islanders from all around the Pacific, South Seas and Melanesia where they lived as a true community and a place of peace and harmony when it had been populated.

So why did they leave?

Further back there were prolific island gardens growing all manner of foods not commonly known in Western supermarkets. Did you know that there is a multitude of varieties of bananas and some you have to cook? Then there were yams, taro, cassava and all varieties of vegetables and fruit trees including the Wongai, the Torres Strait plum tree, a true delicacy and other exotic tropical fruit most people never get to see.

What was remarkable was that these food gardens were abandoned!

Out in the bay you could reach into the water and pluck a fish out of the water with your hand, that's how thick they were and I'm not exaggerating. I don't know about the world of now or how much we have damaged it irreversibly but then when I was there such pockets were still prolific, abundant and free.

So why were there no people living at this idyllic tropical paradise?!! The more I saw, the more the question stood out in my mind.

Other than some very fat and healthy wild pigs and birdlife helping themselves there was not a human soul to be seen.

'How very strange,' I thought!

I was finally told that the government had evicted and forcibly moved the people from their own homes and had made them a 'town,' elsewhere as we travelled to a place in the desert to visit them.

We found them cooped up in little tin huts surrounded with a barbed wire fence around it, miserably unhappy.

From 1924 to 1967 the Lockhart River Mission was run by the Anglican Church before the people were kicked out. They were obviously too happy apart from the rat race and hatred cannot bear to witness happiness.

Banned from visiting their home with all the high nutrition that proliferated there, the overlords had provided the people with white flour, white sugar, cheap alcohol in the form of methylated spirits and for any slave labour that was imposed, they rewarded them with the addictive substance of tobacco.

I could not believe the spiteful victimisation.

The 'reservation' looked like those concentration camps that you see in black and white movies except it was in the middle of the desert. The metal huts were too hot. How to oppress and torment a people.

"To what end," I questioned?

When you work too hard to create a ghetto it is only natural that depression will follow the dispossession. When you deprive people of basic freedoms and natural privileges people become sad and ill.

I saw what I saw. It was there. It was not good.

In those days at this man made hell, Islanders were still cooking on wood fires, used kerosene pressure lanterns and had no electricity, no refrigerators, no cooking stoves and no sewage systems. They were constrained to shit in buckets and then carry those buckets away to manually dispose of the contents in the desert because they could no longer make compost having been disallowed from their gardens!

188

But why? To what end?

The history of how the Islanders were exploited and the resources of the Torres Strait looted in so many ways fills volumes. You will find it in the history section of any good library around the world.

Some of the young boys had gotten into the methylated spirits and thoroughly intoxicated, had harmed a young girl who was being attended to by the older women. The Elders were distraught. They were in a dilemma. If they reported to the white police they feared they would never see their sons again and so decided on traditional law.

When things had settled as much as possible one old man went to a secret hiding place and dug up and unwrapped a miniature model sailing boat about two metres long that the Islanders often used to race for fun. It was a common pastime.

He wept in memory of how they were now no longer permitted to go to the beach and play with these recreational toys to sail and race them and be entertained, as they had always done, for fear of being jailed!
This did not sit well. Something was terribly wrong here!

The special rules made for these good people... they could not fish, they could not go to the gardens to tend them and collect food, they could not hunt the wild pig, or cultivate domestic ones or chickens, they could not sail the model sailing boats and so many other things. The penalty they feared was Palm Island, a jail reserved for Islanders and Aboriginals still in place today.

Needless to say, I was enraged. We provided them with victuals and produce from their own gardens and bringing them flowers which they were too frightened to arrange in case they got caught revealing aesthetic reminders of their once held freedoms.

It was bizarre!

We hunted and caught some wild pigs which we roasted for their benefit. They needed protein as they were deprived and emaciated.

Extremely grateful but fearful of getting caught eating food they thought was banned to them, they hardly ate.

For a few days we stayed there and for a part of this time I had remained on the boat to cook. Later, we adopted a wild piglet from this place and this piglet became the boat mascot. It grew until the whole boat tilted to one side and we had to leave it at Thursday Island. Let me tell you, pigs are more intelligent than dogs but that will be for another story.

We had to continue on our journey so we left them well provided, said our farewells and went back to the boat. On the way, with immense sadness I took time to briefly scrutinise the gumtree and paperbark cathedral which was starting to become dilapidated.

Their solace, their religious freedom had also been taken away. The level of cruelty that had been visited here was unprecedented.

The night before we left, Eddie was weeping and telling the story of how he wanted to win proper land rights for his people. In those days of affliction he was considered to be a daydreamer by so many both black and white who thought only of impossibilities and were resigned to an unnecessary fate.

He was a pioneer ahead of his time!

It took Eddie over twenty-one years to win back Islander Land Rights but he went on and did it. The rest is history. The story of Eddie Mabo is well known. He did exactly what he set out to do: Fulfil Natural Justice and Human Rights for his people…

It was a long and protracted battle. One of many chapters on this convoluted roller coaster of events was described to me. If I recall correctly how it was told to me, something like this happened:

One day the representatives of the Crown came to Mer, Murray Island, preparing to conclude they had won the ability to continue to deprive an ancient race of their island home and natural birthrights.

The judge was beginning to make his closing argument in which he included something like, "Commonwealth law requires written documentation as evidence of possession of proprietary rights which has not been provided.." Or something like that.

A very old man held his hand up but was ignored. I think it may have been Passi. He tried to speak but was asked to keep quiet because court was in session. His representing lawyer then petitioned the court for leave to introduce vital evidence of immense import and leave was granted.

The old man was humoured. After all, what could they possibly bring?

The old man was questioned and he said, "We do indeed have written documentation of our laws and our regulations."

The terms of reference already in place… "Can you produce them?" The question was asked and he answered, "Yes, I can." The old man was given time to go to a secret place to fetch the ancient parchment.

It was carefully examined upon delivery. Upon this scroll, the skin of an animal, there in plain sight for all to see, was written Malo's Laws going back thousands of years before Moses, that had been inscribed and hidden and also handed down orally through the generations!

I do not know if this incident happened exactly like this. I was not there at that point in time. This simplistic rendition, if it happened could have been but one small part of many episodes in that long story. The actual case, over long time, was complicated and difficult and dealt with intricate matters, the byways of return to the golden rule each time it is sought to be circumvented!

It turned out the Islanders were not at first having a dispute with the government but each other, over pre-existing borders as they had since they first implemented their rights of possession many thousands of years ago. They would encroach, dispute, resolve and argue and fight over who owned what and where. Unbeknown to themselves this matched the very precedent already set by Commonwealth Law. For that matter, plain common sense!

Malo's Law was now finally vindicated. Or was it? There were complex and intricate twists and turns in this matter too long to describe here.. and then... all appeared lost when there was an appeal. The case was not closed. The matter was opened and would continue.

Another protracted legal tug-of-war ensued.

More time and attrition and the matter was churned some more... If justice was to be seen to be done...

To cut a very long story short, on 3rd June 1992 the High Court of Australia recognised that Torres Strait Islanders held ownership of their land. In acknowledging the traditional rights of Islanders to their land the court held that Indigenous Australians have proprietary rights to land in a legal form of ownership referred to as, "Native Title," which exists for all Indigenous people based on pre-existing traditional law. The following year the Commonwealth Native Title Act 1993 was passed through the Australian Parliament. This opened the way for claims by Aboriginal and Torres Strait Islander peoples to their traditional rights over their own land.

Eddie died before he got his land, if at all, but he managed to set a precedent for all others. A form of justice was done! An accomodation was arrived at. The acknowledgement of traditional customs and land rights.

It took twenty-one years!

There are many aspects… *"The Court declared that the Meriam people were entitled as against the whole world to possession…"*

And that the litigants, the Islanders, *"… had shown an effective system of title where individual lots of land handed down from one generation to the next, including cultivation of these lots by families and individuals…"*

"Entitlement to possession, occupation and use of lands through customary land title …"

And of course the acknowledgement of.. *Human Rights!*

The Torres Strait Islanders had been administering their laws, property rights and culture well for many thousands of years with Malo ra Gelar long before….

Some six months after Eddie had died at only age 55, a panel of judges decided the obvious in favour of Natural Justice. This became the 'Mabo Law' for land rights which was a milestone not only in human rights but in the rights of traditional owners everywhere.

Eddie was buried in the cemetery at Townsville in 1992 and I was there when the Islander traditional ceremony of unveiling his tombstone was carried out.

In 1995 some vandals desecrated Eddie's grave and defaced it. More sadness was underfoot.

After that, a decision was made and his remains were taken back home to his beloved Mer, Murray Island, to the land of his birth where he was given a proper and fully traditional burial.

He had fought the good fight and won! His wonderful family had supported him for many long years through his battle for justice.

Like so many heroes throughout history the attrition of that battle caused him to pay the ultimate price but in the end it was no longer in dispute that this was somebody's land indeed and that so called, 'nullius' existed only in the bereft souls of the pillaging invaders.

It was the land of the people of this realm as it had been for countless thousands of years.

"They are our laws. We have Malo Ra Gelar. It says that Malo keeps to his own place; Malo does not trespass in another man's property. Malo keeps his hands to himself. He does not touch what is not his. He does not permit his feet to carry him towards other men's property. His hands are not grasping. He holds them back. He does not wander from his path. He walks on tip-toe, silent and careful, leaving no signs to tell that this is the way he took." David Passi recounting an aspect of Malo Ra Gelar.

For over 200 years Torres Strait Islanders and their resources had been plundered and exploited and they were forced to remain self-reliant subsisting only on what they could produce themselves by their own efforts. Torres Strait Islanders were not included as citizens of Queensland or indeed Australia until after the 1967 Referendum and even after that they were not treated equally.

34. Beach Girls

Paul could tell a story better than the best... anecdotes, events, jokes and narratives of ancient past abounded. He had an endless repertoire of didactic tales to tell and his upbeat humour was captivating.

He could sit around the fire and entertain better than any movie or sports event and people loved it.

Sometimes the storytelling would get him into trouble because the young ladies would like to follow him like groupies.

There was no television in the islands in those days.

One day a mixed group had been following him up the beach in droves to hear tales of times gone by. As they jovially strolled by, some older women became irritated assuming nasty thoughts and started backbiting among themselves.

Once around the island and then back, the stories were proliferating and the group was getting bigger to the disappointment of the dried up gossipers.

At the end of the day the crowd went home and Paul came back to the boat where we resumed preparing for the next fishing trip.

He had broken the mould of what was considered by some to be expected behaviour but of course the loudest had broken bigger taboos in secret so they made much noise casting stones of intolerance around to distract from their own peccadillos.

It had all started with a tale about how the 'boss man' had told a boy who could hardly speak English.

"Go to the 'marina' (a jetty for mooring boats) and when you see the supply boat arrive, quickly run back and tell me." The boss man wanted to be the first to buy the cargo.

He didn't hear from the boy and saw the boat leaving, meaning it had unloaded and sold the cargo. Realising he had lost the financial advantage he had sought, he angrily went to the marina, found the boy sitting there and chastised him. "Well, what happened? The boat arrived and you didn't tell me. Why not?

The boy said, "Well, I waited for the submarina, but no submarina came!"

He had misunderstood the word 'marina.'

That story led to another and another and so on until it opened up a shitload of great stories as if they would never end and as you know when there's a good audience the performance shines.

Not all the stories were that funny but it was the way he told them that lent a certain humour about life and where there's laughter people would want to gather and to stay to hear the next.

The best part was that unlike television there were no dumb commercials to interrupt the flow of entertainment!

35. Darnley Deep

Tropical cyclones are a common feature of the North Queensland and Torres Strait Region.

There are few places where stillness resides during a cyclone. One of these is the centre of the cyclone but that safety is gone when the periphery moves past you with all its natural fury.

A cave high in the hills is a possibility if you can find one. The deep ocean is still another and it too has use.

Understanding makes the difference.

When a cyclone hits, there is often much destruction and people who do not know what to do, among other things, lose their boats.

Old Pop Barunah would tell me many stories of the 'old days.' From 1965 to about 1969 when I was often in town at Port Douglas in-between jobs Pop and I would sit, chat and partake of tea and scones with jam whiling away the time that had suddenly become plentiful now that I was away from the bustle of a city.

He would recount the events of those 'old times.' Among other things, Pop had been a Master Maritime Pilot on many a vessel navigating the reefs safely for his employers.

During World War II, despite not being recognised as citizens almost every able-bodied Indigenous man throughout the Torres Strait Islands signed up to defend Australia against the threat of invasion.

Pop was one of them. He served in The Torres Strait Light Infantry Battalion of the Australian Army... but that's another story.... He would regularly tell me of the many thousands of years old, 'Malo Ra Gelar' this being Malo's Law and of land disputes and how they were resolved. It was the first time I would hear of how important this ancient law-book was to Islanders. How ownership was marked with 'elikup,' boundary markers and of Malo and his uncle Bomai who were ancient leaders and how Malo had brought the law a very long time ago.

He would describe how disputes were managed with diplomacy and discussion in council meetings first.

Pop spoke strongly about traditional land tenure rules and inheritance laws and how all the people respected the ancestral tenets going back to the 'stone age' as he put it.

He would explain in his own way how the topography and the arrangement of the natural features of an area would be identified with the 'elikup' which were carefully maintained to determine which Islander or family group owned which plot of land. It impressed me greatly that the land markings were in accordance with the actual lay of the land instead of one dimensional straight lines that miss so much...

He would tell me how Gelar, the law, was respected, observed and maintained in a manner clearly identifiable to all and how it was applied to all property, be this specific family garden plots where food was grown, material which was stored, seafaring vessels, fish traps and more; and how everyone respected it and that penalties for breaches could be severe especially in older times.

He would tell of Bomai-Malo ceremonies and dances and how they had been banned by the Australian government along with the use of indigenous languages and dialects including Erubim-Mìr and Meriam-Mir of the eastern group, Kalaw-Lagaw-Ya of the central islands and Kala Kawa Ya of top western and western islands.

With a cheeky grin he told that they would speak their languages in secret anyway.

Time and again Pop would proudly and reverently recount Malo's Property Law from memory: *"Malo tag mauki mauki, Teter mauki mauki. Malo tag aorir aorir,*

Teter aorir aorir. Malo tag tupamait tupamait, Teter tupamait tupamait." Translated, "Malo keeps his hands to himself; he does not touch what is not his. He does not permit his feet to carry him towards another man's property. His hands are not grasping, he holds them back. He does not wander from his path. He works on tiptoe, silent, careful, leaving no sign to tell that this is the way he took."

And the Decree Against Theft; *"Arokak arokak lug-ise waipedawa. Deregkak deregkak lug-ise waipedawa."* Meaning, "You would not pluck fruit which was not fit to be eaten. What does not belong to you is as unattractive as the unripe fruit you would shun."

Also about Duty; *"Gaka nakariklu Usiami gab ge a Segi gab ge."* To mean, "Stars travel their own paths across the sky. I cannot walk the path that is Usiam's, nor can I walk the path that is Seg's." In other words: Perform your assigned duty, clean up behind yourself, live your own life, attend to your business… and other precepts I can no longer remember. These were inscribed long ago and written down, then hidden in secret places known only to high initiates of the Bomai-Malo community.

Pop would tell how they could communicate from island to island without radio but internal means. How the Zogo-le could heal and how the Maaid-le sorcerers could take over birds and other animals to observe or sharks to attack enemies and how poison dust was put on butterflies' wings and released into the house of an enemy while he was sleeping and more... and how Bomai and Malo brought the law to regulate and control the previous lawlessness.

Being young I barely paid attention to the serious stuff for I enjoyed the tales of things that had happened in the adventures and the upbeat humour that he brought to these histories.

One such tale was how they saved the pearling luggers during one of the worst cyclones, Cyclone Mahina in 1899. History tells how Cyclone Mahina was the deadliest cyclone in recorded Australian history and the most intense tropical cyclone ever recorded in the Southern Hemisphere.

Mahina struck Bathurst Bay, Cape York Peninsula and Queensland on March the 4th 1899 and its winds and enormous storm surges killed more than 300 people.

Pearling luggers were prolific during that time. The pearling industry was in full force and at risk of being decimated if they lost the lugger boats. A lugger is a gaff-rigged two masted ketch built from timber. They were usually 45 to 60 feet long with a low draft and usually no bulwarks. This was to facilitate diving.

With their elegant curves, especially when in full sail, luggers are a great sight. A joy to sail, they are silent and cut the water smoothly. Some years later when I participated on a trip on the *'Torres Herald'* a fifty footer, it was the most comfortable marine vessel I had ever experienced. Totally silent, it cut the waters ever so smoothly... it was a meditative joy to sail unhurriedly upon it.

Pop would tell me at length how the legendary 'Darnley Deep' was in some places 40 fathoms or deeper. That is about 240 feet! Legendary? Well, more infamous than legendary. Those 'deeps' had cost the lives of too many a young pearl diver because of greedy slave drivers!

I first heard the original name of the region, "Lumudhal," and its oceanic peripheries of, "Koey" at the East and, "Badu Hoki" at the West from Pop. These designations had important connotations to the traditional mariners.

In great detail, ol' Pop would explain how pearling divers were reliant on the tenders above who manned the pump with the air tube feeding into their helmets. That was all that was keeping them alive and providing them with air to breathe. And how in the early days pearls were common. When he was a ten year old child he would pick up pearl shells on the beach.

There was massive abundance before the mass exploitation came. Children played marbles with huge pearls as they could easily be found even in shallow waters. Not all were white or cream but also black and pink and blue having no value to the locals because they were so common. The curious bauble colours were attractive to child like minds but real people were focussed on food and husbanding the environments which enabled life in a challenging climate.

Pop would tell me how visible environmental change had been upsetting the delicate balance of nature in the region when he was a little boy and how his Elders were becoming concerned at changes they could notice even back then. (The contaminants of the industrial revolution [1760 to 1830] were, even then, dispersing around the planet similarly to the way that the Chernobyl disaster (26 April 1986) has altered us all in more recent times.)

Even now as I write this, changes are adversely affecting the Torres Strait and the low-lying islands are sinking beneath the water. Who is listening? Who cares? Who is paying attention? Who is concerned?

He would explain how by 1871 a diving suit had been developed that allowed access down to 20 fathoms. So the bastards pushed them twice that far.

As exploitation increased and pearl shells became harder to find, the divers were forced to dive to increasingly greater depths. By the end of the 1930s, some divers were going down to 40 fathoms at immense risk to themselves in areas such as Darnley Deep. The bends killed many as did snagging on rocks and becoming trapped at great depths.

Pop must have been in his 90's when I last saw him. He was still powerfully muscled like a lean version of Arnold Schwarzenegger, abs and all, a superb athlete who would uproot trees to clear ground for the planting of manioc/cassava and yams and food bearing crops. Indeed I helped him for a while and he could work all day long, non-stop clearing, preparing and planting. The result was a prolific abundance of food for the whole extended family!

Ol' Pop the Great Elder would say, "The world is there, the rest is up to the person... all the ingredients already exist and the rest is up to you! The possibilities are endless..." Sometimes he would speak of more profound subjects and explained that the environments which form the life support systems of our world are not separate from us but are the other 99.99% of our existence. He was concerned at the changes he had witnessed and of those to come.. I came to understand clearly that if we separate ourselves from, or damage those foundational life supporting systems that we as sparks on the surface of this planet rely upon, we would cease to exist. When we one day come to choose to enhance the environments then the environments will enhance our existence. Damage the environmental life support systems and we damage all life forms including the most fragile and recent of them all, the human, ourselves. Disease, war, pestilence and destruction then follows. He was immensely concerned at the ignorance of those men who wilfully destroy life to gather money, a mere measuring tool. Life will continue but humans being the latest short lived evolutionary bump and a fragile mass of habit patterns who make too many bad choices and place humanity's future in the balance, may not. Under the surface the rest of our existence remains unseen, the survival senses being a minuscule fragment of an awesome and vast range of possibilities. Natural people live a little more inside of Great Nature's immense spectrum, not merely on the surface and of necessity understand a bit more of what is behind the appearance. Even though the Great Ones have a vaster than average span of control, it is minute in the face of a limitless intelligence controlling more than we can see on the surface of life... for little creatures such as us, our heart, circulation, breath, digestion and the functions of the organs that enable life and mobility, sentience and consciousness which differentiates humans from a rock are beyond our control. The quality of our consciousness is vital because with it we can create heavens or hells on earth depending on how we combine things.

Having the opportunity to interact in relationship with existence in different ways, what little we can do should be conducted with respect for all that which enables life as we know it. Tar and cement cannot produce oxygen or much else that gives or enables life... All the ingredients are here! Heaven or hell is what we make... what we can make! Most of it is done for us and all we have to do is to arrange things well and leave those things alone that should not be tampered with...."

Understanding the difference is the key which allows us to leave a pleasant legacy for future generations... and so much more! They were good talks.

When he spoke of these subjects I would go into a reverie like state and travel inwardly with him to other dimensions looking clearly down upon the Earth with deeper understanding...

When I later returned to the city I found that consciousness of environmental conservation and inner human potential was beginning to emerge in a nascent state. It was to grow somewhat over the years but in some corners it would do so with massive resistance.

One day Pop told me of the day they saved a whole fleet of pearling luggers by sinking them!

When in March of 1899 notice came that a cyclone was approaching, this is what they did. There was not much time. They took their vessels to Darnley Deep and sank them! This saved the boats.

Let me explain: A sea-cock is a valve in the hull of a watercraft used for letting in water either to clean the bilges, flood the ballast or scuttle a vessel.

To save the large boats and the pearling luggers during cyclones, despite the scepticism and complaints of those who did not understand, the Islanders would save their boats by opening the sea-cock and sinking the vessel somewhere deep where the waters remain still, unaffected by the storm on the agitated surface.

Places such as Darnley Deep were ideal for this.

And so they did. Those who listened to the Islanders saved their boats but those who 'knew better' if they could find anything left of their wrecks, the remains were as good as toothpicks smashed up on the rocks and shores and reefs.

208

When the cyclone was over, the Islanders would dive down, seal the openings in the vessel and pump it full of air sufficiently so that the air would cause the vessel to float again. The rest was then elbow grease bailing out the water.

Many a pearling lugger was saved in this way in the 'good old days.'

I did not have the fortune to have been able to participate in such an exercise as I heard from old Pop but I never forgot. Just in case!

Islanders have improved and mastered risk mitigation over many millennia in this dangerous realm and they have always been forward thinking in skills of taking action to prevent or reduce disaster.

This and much more was told to me by Pop Barunah...

36. Eggs and Plums

We mainly lived off the sea where food was abundant. For curry, shoyu, tea and tinned stuff we would get supplies from the Chinese supermarket. Such items as knives, cooking utensils, matches, kero, lamps and the like we got from Burns Philp store. After stocking up on essential victuals to supplement the trip we would load the boat and depart.

Some of the guys stayed at the pub too long and missed the boat.

Daily fare was mainly pescatarian diet. Sometimes we simply had to stay out longer because fishing was sparse. On such occasions when the going got tough, the tough went looking for eggs and plums.

Along the eastern coastline of Australia the Wongai plum trees grew wild as well as yams often growing as big as a small car.

In the right season there were turtle eggs. Turtle eggs are identical to the size of ping-pong balls but with a soft skin. When hard boiled they are the same as chicken eggs and extremely nutritious. A good high protein food for the price of digging in the sand.

If the season was right there were also the Gainau pigeons and their smaller eggs. Gainau are the Torres Strait pigeon (Carpophaga lutuaosa).

Coconuts grew wild and provided water, the green ones gave a bitter sweet perfect hydration fluid better than any soft drink or those unhealthy so called 'sports drinks' laden with white sugar and chemicals. The meat and pulp of the coconut depending on the stage of its development could be simply eaten as a nut either raw or roasted or the scraped meat could be turned into milk for cooking curry.

Some places had mangoes growing wild. Usually there would be pigs around there, wild pigs which had to be cooked very well.

Some fish or another could always be caught as they were plentiful in those days. In some places at other seasons there were immense outcrops where sea birds would lay their eggs and these tasted good also. Eggs are eggs.

During one rough anomalous season things got so bad that we actually had to eat the catch, crayfish tail, which was not a good idea to indulge too much. Wild crayfish are considered a delicacy in cities. Like many oceanic creatures crayfish are mainly eaters of the shit of other fish and eating them too much or too often can give rise to boils where there is insufficient vitamin C in the diet.

In any event boat life requires supplementation with vitamin C and prolonged trips can give rise to scurvy. Being also the cook I introduced pineapple juice since lemons and citrus fruit were hard to find in the region.

The pineapple juice became so popular that some of the crew began stealing it from stock so after a few trips I'd had enough of it. I then purchased bulk but assigned several tins to each individual and marked them with his name instead of keeping stock, making it each individual's personal responsibility. No more thefts occurred after that.

It's not so easy to starve where there is no manufactured lack. The economy of nature is always super abundant and in excess. It varies but Nature is generous even in hard times. We took only that which was needed and no more. Perhaps a little more for tomorrow!

Oh yes, there is skill and effort involved but there were no couch potatoes then. Such would have starved. Everyone contributed.

37. What Type of Karate Is That?

When the giant fishing trawlers from Japan moored at Thursday Island one of the first things they did was to lay tatami on the huge decks and go hell for leather; judo, newaza et al. When there was no time to lay mats it would be kendo or karate-do. It was pleasant to watch and learn but when they noticed us watching they would try to hide what they were doing.

They did not like strangers watching their practice. I had heard that there was a dojo at T.I. but I never got around to it. Besides, I don't consider casual training to be worth more than a head trip. We were mostly out at sea and not usually very long at T.I.

Practice has to be daily in order to bring about the transformation required to hone preconditioned responses, good coordination and skill. For now the ocean would be my dojo and what a Dojo it was!

Land was a different and complementary experience. After you adjusted your sea legs and washed off the salt it was a dimension in itself. I found the ocean more honest and safer.

It was a tradition on Thursday night after the cabaret for the local drunks to brawl. The white guys who hung about after closing time usually got beaten up half to death. The hospital expected casualties on Thursday nights. I guess it was the way some deluded fellows thought would get back at the invaders or something like that, not realising that there is no colour to alcoholics and that these were probably drunks for the same reason that they were, despair and because they felt equally as downtrodden, often of their own making.

Of course the drunken brawlers never went near a Japanese man whether he was sober or drunk. They had learnt that the hard way.

One night I had stayed out too long and the drunks were pouring out of the pubs. I was talking to some attractive girls. Suddenly, on impulse, I turned around and punched the air behind me.

Instead of air, my fist found a button, the chin of a guy with a four by two club, about to hit me on the head. He went to sleep immediately.

I am not sure why it happened and always wondered about that impulse. What caused me to hit what I thought was the air behind me? I tried to rationalise it; perhaps I had, 'subconsciously' seen his reflection in the girl's eyes or their facial expression but it was dark with only meagre street lighting. Most likely it was Sensei Sugano's Ushiro Waza training. I guess I'll never know.

Then this fellow's mates arrived, the girls took off and I had an interesting situation on my hands.

A Japanese man on the footpath stood with his hands in his pockets and watched the whole event which only lasted a few minutes. When it was over I went back to the boat. The fight was a pretty standard Jiyu-Waza situation and a non-event. They had no skill and tripped over each other but I found myself quizzing over the earlier rear attack response. It was not a conscious effort. It happened at the right instant! Why?

Sometime after that event I noticed that there was what appeared to be a karate dojo adjacent to where the fight had taken place. Standing there confident and relaxed was the same guy who had watched the fight earlier.

This time he was standing on the open veranda wearing a gi. A handsome, short Japanese gentleman he was and by the way that he carried himself, extremely fit. By extremely fit I mean athletic. He glided when he walked and looked like he could do just about anything despite his age.

I could see the interior of the dojo through the large double doors. In the building there were young men in gi's, the beginners practising kata to one side, instructors barking orders and counting loudly as in unison they performed the relevant action to the count ...... ichi! ni!

san! shi! go! roku! sichi! hatchu! ku! juuuuuuu... whilst the more experienced performing kumite at the other side of the dojo. Hajimeeee! and they would spar. Yammeeee! and they would bow and resume sitting in seiza in an orderly line while others stood, bowed and resumed activity on command.

The smell of the dojo, bamboo, hessian, gi's, sweat... was another homecoming.

It felt good and threatening at the same time and the energy here was very intense. I stood for a while observing carefully to see what techniques I could steal. Normally this practice hall was closed but today the main doors were left open. It was a very hot day.

"Do you mind if I watch?" I asked gratuitously as I had already been watching.

He grunted ambiguously. No facial expression. But I could see that he was studying me in his peripheral vision. I kept the right maai as was my habit. No reason. He was as ready as I but it was clear he was not a foe whilst there was no doubt that he was a warrior measuring me as I measured him.

I asked him, "Do you accept students?"

He grunted again, still looking ahead and past me as if disdainfully. Characteristically still no facial expression. I'm never sure how to take that. I think it's an old Samurai thing, generations of casehardened poker face gives away nothing. Zero or minimal eye contact. Also traditional.

Somehow I had a feeling he didn't like caucasians much but I may have been wrong and perhaps it was simply the way he was.

"If I were interested in training could I train in between trips because I am a fisherman? What kind of karate-do you do here?" I asked awkwardly.

He replied smiling or grimacing, I'm not sure which... "Kyokushin here we do." Then he asked. "What kind karate you?"

I didn't quite get the question at first. "I beg your pardon?" I replied.

He continued to stare straight ahead without expression. I stood and waited respectfully. I was not going into the dojo without his consent. He seemed to have seniority and I got the impression that those doing the instructing were his senior students and he was the Sensei.

I continued to wait. He continued to stand. And then almost imperceptibly the corner of his lower eyelid turned up only slightly and a gleam appeared in his eyes.

The activity inside suddenly stopped and everybody sat in Zazen. A very intense quiet pervaded, cutting the atmosphere with an almost cruel purity which I found nourishing,

It looked like he was making a stoic effort to speak again and didn't really want to interrupt the silence.

At the sound of a clap those inside all got up, bowed toward the kamiza, the instructors and then each other and departed by way of an entrance at the other side of the building. Class over!

I could feel the big buildup of energy but with an unmistakable hint of emphasis he finally got it out, "What kind karate you?"

"Why do you ask?" I replied finally understanding the question.

He replied, "I don't sink you need we Karate! You crean up several azza day. What kind karate you?"

I was not sure whether to take that as a rejection or a backhanded compliment, or both!

"I like to practice," I replied.

"Ahh soo," finally what looked like a smile or it could've been a grimace but I think it was more like a smile. "You fishing. Prenty big dojo. Me pearl diver before.." and then a definite smile.

It was overdue time to answer his question. In those days I was a bit jealous of my art. It was reflex action as a result of good instruction and dedicated training. I had not analysed regressive ideas such as, 'styles.' Not wishing to divulge the secrets of Aiki Jutsu or the fact that all natural movement is simply efficiency, economy of motion, physics in action when you let go and unleash the innate potential, so I simply said "Oh, I made it up."

"No biriv you," he smiled cheekily.

Being young, impatient and busy, this largely tacit conversation looked like taking forever, so I decided to go back to my chores and skip whatever challenge he was imposing, if any. If this was a test of patience I chose to fail it. Watching grass grow has never been my forté although there must be some merit in it for I hear that the great Kublai Khan did that most of the time and the rest of the time he won battles and helped build civilisation.

I replied, "It's been good to make your acquaintance. Please have a good day," I bowed slightly and respectfully.

He nodded the shorter bow of a Senpai* letting me know that he considered me Kohai.* That was okay with me.

With nothing else to say or do, I left. I would have liked to have trained at length with this fellow. I had a feeling that he had much to offer but it was not to be. He imparted much and I learnt a lot in that short meeting.

After that, any time we were on land at T.I. for any brief time and I had occasion to walk past his Dojo, if he was there he would nod his head slightly with a wry smile and walk back inside.

I would nod back and keep walking. There was an understanding!

In Japan, the relationship between senpai (先輩, "senior") and kōhai (後輩, "junior") is an interpersonal hierarchical relationship defining societal roles.

38. Mascot

Mascot was a pig who became the boat mascot when we were at the then banned Lockhart River Mission site. We had hunted wild pigs to vary our diet and supply the poor souls who had been relegated to a reservation in the desert for no good reason other than they had been too happy on the coast with its immense natural abundance.

We gathered food from their now neglected and prolific food gardens which the previously domestic pigs, now gone wild, were now glutting on.

Not programmed to miss an opportunity to get the food nature offered, the Islander crew took this abundance of pork as a blessing. The people in the reservation finally got to feast on well cooked protein to which they had been held in fear to go and access themselves.

In that hunt along the beach one of the piglets escaped and started swimming. I felt sorry for it as the sharks would have surely got it. I was cooking on the boat at the time and saw what happened and before the crew could capture it and most likely kill it, I dived into the water and rescued the little thing. It squealed and complained a lot at first as piglets do. I made a brew from powdered milk and found a way to feed it then wrapped it in a blanket, swayed it gently and it soon settled down.

I made a case for it being a lucky charm! Not having much meat on it because of its size there was at least temporary agreement.

The talk was of growing it and fattening it for food later on. As time went by 'Mascot' as we named the piglet became such a good friend that nobody had the heart to consider that any more.

Besides it was believed by most that Mascot was bringing us good luck! Our catch had never been so prolific and everyone was doing well. Soon the 'lucky charm' belief took hold very firmly.

The pig was to be protected as a friend and that was that! Over quite a few trips we fed Mascot soft boiled crayfish heads and it grew to a very large size. It was not long before Mascot was huge and heavy. Too huge and too heavy to continue living on the boat.

Pigs are much more intelligent than dogs and they understand language. Mascot knew what we were up to, it knew when we were going out, it knew what we were talking about and it walked around the boat deck as if it owned the place.

Mascot had great sea legs and enjoyed it when the boat was travelling, lying sprawled upon the deck with a happy smile upon its face.

Once adopted as the boat mascot nobody thought of harming the porker. They were protective for it was said that it would bring bad luck to harm our good luck charm. Of course!

Every time food was on the horizon Mascot happily grunted. It loved to graze on fish offcuts and oceanic abundance that we shared with it. Not to mention the leftover rice or damper and other tidbits. Over time Mascot grew so big that when we went on a fishing trip the boat would tilt too much because Mascot favoured one side of the boat or the other as there was not enough space for the now large pig in the middle where the freezer box was situated. Imagine a motor vessel tilting like a yacht tacking into the wind!

Eventually it became ridiculous and could pose some problems in a storm and so reluctantly and sadly we had to leave our friend with relatives in Tamwai town.

Mascot understood this too and wept. The boat had become its home. Some of the crew hid a tear as well. Mascot was our friend.

For a long time we were busy fishing. Then when we came back one day, we were sad to find that Mascot was gone. The story that was told was that in our absence it had escaped its pen and tried to swim to Hammond Island and the sharks got it.

We were heartbroken, not only because Mascot had been our lucky charm but because its jolly and happy personalty was no longer with us.

When Mascot had been with us, we experienced our largest catches and made good money one and all and none of the crew had loud disagreements in case the pig noticed and it brought bad luck.

Now Mascot was gone!

39. Drum

Sometimes in life when saving or protecting another life, it necessitates that you put your own life a little in harm's way. Some say that to be vigilant is overprotective but isn't prevention better than the long, hard road to patching up the mess that follows stupid behaviour?

Contingency thinking is a good thing. It prevents accidents. When proper preparation is left out, sometimes we as humans find out the hard way and the lesson can be a lifetime of pain. Whilst blaming is the cause of depression, taking responsibility the source of self-mastery even if it is a long climb back. Erring on the side of caution is preferable but not always possible, so I have to take responsibility for my decision of what happened next. It certainly slowed me down after that.

Thursday Island wharf. Very low tide. Laziness, womanising, drunkenness and other lack of discipline brought about this unusual condition.

Everybody was running late. The tide beat us this time. My job was to guard the boat but I could not do it alone and so I waited. Normally Paul does not wait for laggards. With him there is a tide in the affairs of men which must be taken at the flood and will lead on to fortune... or else you get left behind. Well, this was that one rare occasion when it was omitted and the shallows and the miseries were looming up ahead. More than I could ever imagine.

To cut a long story short, it was getting choppy and the mother boat was unhappily and uncomfortably swaying hard from side to side whilst alongside the end of Thursday Island jetty.

It was a very low tide. The wind was up and rising. Finally some crew arrived late. Conditions were not fit for loading a boat and getting worse. There was a big storm brewing and we were urgently packing cargo and equipment for the trip. It is better to be out at sea than in an unprotected harbour in a storm and we needed to get the hell out of there.

Paul had disappeared on some chore or another and had asked Mark to get a block and tackle wherewith to load the boat. To put Mark in charge was not a good idea; not even at the best of times. Mark was not only ignorant but also lazy when it came to doing productive work. As usual he failed to do what he had been told and managed to find a plain block to lower the heavy goods. Not wise. In other words, there would be no fulcrum to take the weight of heavy things.

A block and tackle is a device arranged where a rope is threaded through more than one pulley so that the weight is now suspended by two or more pulleys rather than one. This means the weight is split equally between several pulleys so each one holds a portion of the weight thereby distributing the load making it easier to haul the rope. In such a way you only have to apply the amount of force divided by the number of pulleys.

For example if there are two pulleys the distance of the rope will be twice as long, the force has been divided in half but the distance that the rope must be pulled has doubled. Whilst you do have to pull on more length of rope, the extra time is worth it because it gives you more control and greater safety.

If you haven't seen one, a picture or the real item describes it better than words.

We did not have the right equipment because in trying to take a shortcut the lazy bastard did not bother to go and find one.

What followed was to spell the final chapter of my adventures in the Torres Strait.

The possibility of a mishap was entirely foreseeable. I cautioned Mark to find the right equipment, the block and tackle, or leave the loading for another time or at least wear gloves but being frantic, arrogant and hung over he went ahead anyway.

As usual Mark wanted to make his mark and as usual it was to be another scar on the landscape of life. I should have walked away but instead I got back onto the deck of the boat to help the crew there. The going was tough and I am not a shirker.

We loaded the lighter stuff. That went okay. Then it came time for the fuel drums. Two 44 gallon drums full of diesel. These weigh a bit over 300 pounds or 137 kilos. Having no gloves the rope slipped and burned his hands so with total disregard for consequences Mark let go and the drum hurtled down about to land on David.

Some people say that I should have stepped to one side and let the young man die and protect myself. When the rope slipped from Mark and his helper's hands, the 44 gallon drum full of diesel fuel started sliding down at speed. In its trajectory was a young man who had recently joined the crew. He would have been crushed to death or worse, severely injured.

David, not his traditional name, was a quiet soul, a timid and gentle Kuka-Kuka boy. It was said that he was being hunted by his own countrymen and that they wanted to punish him for refusing to eat human flesh.

He was hiding with us. He was a good person. Paul was happy to offer him protection. He was a hard worker, quiet, non-argumentative and kept to himself. The Torres strait was a safe haven. Any uninvited Papuan man would have stood out like dogs' balls and been identified immediately. There were a few New Guinea people here but they had been invited and were from the friendly tribes where they had relatives and kinship connections. All good.

David was alone. As for the others, the attempted invaders, from time immemorial whether it was Kebisu from the Western Islands and his ancestors; or Dabad from the eastern group and his ancestors, the Torres Strait had for thousands of years regularly trounced invaders from ancient Papua attempting to set foot into the Torres Strait territories with bad intent. That's the way it was. War!

On the other hand there also existed strong family bonds with some tribes.

On the spur of that moment I could not stand by and watch David get mangled. He was trapped between the pylons of the jetty and the wheelhouse and the trajectory of the drum was headed straight his way with no way of escape.

With boat swaying violently from side to side, he was at risk of getting crushed by the pylons and the boat if he fell off that side, or the drum if he stood there. Because of other stuff that had been dumped along the deck he had nowhere else to go. Bad planning never pays.

As the drum dropped I reflexively stepped forward and temporarily took the weight and redirected it to a safe place away from him. It was the only way at short notice to save the young man. In those unstable conditions I was not properly balanced. He was made safe but immediately I felt an electric bolt of intense pain in my lower back. That sharp pain was indescribable and the inability to move persisted throughout the trip.

In agony I could not work. In excruciating pain for a week I made the decision: Back to Sydney. It was not a hard decision to make. There was no choice. I did not like it but the injury would require treatment not available here.

Catching the drum had been a mistake and a lifetime of pain was to follow but at least my conscience was not hurting.

L5 injury. Disk. Nerve pain. It has been a journey of pain. One of the last emergencies at Torres Strait saw me back in Sydney for a lifetime of Osteopathic, Chiropractic and other treatment.

I went from agile to fragile. Refusing the knife because research showed it was too risky a proposition I embarked on an extremely long and gradual path of pain management to partial recovery

Where is the close shave in this tale? Well, the good news is that I refused an operation after investigating the facts. Too many of one surgeon's patients with L5 problems did not fare any better than before. Many of the people one 'specialist' had operated on had subsequently committed suicide after suffering from the greater pain that he had added to their lives with his guesswork and a sharp implement.

Chronic pain and restricted ability. I learned to work around it. Faking a wellness that I did not entirely have, I compensated by using other strengths. Over time I found ways to manage and correct the condition and go on to a reasonably productive life but it was a long slow path taking many years, with many ups and downs and a measure of disability that I kept hidden as much as possible which was not too hard when among a soft species of mostly academics and pen pushers.

I learnt some important lessons from that drum but would have preferred to take lessons from the Warup Drums of Mer in the Kwod of ancient times instead, where from age ten they produced well rounded, multi-skilled men who could hunt, farm, navigate, protect, build and maintain a viable self-sustaining society. Some were selected to be educated as litigious diplomats keeping the peace in the region.

In some ways, it could be said that through the osmosis of association, I had been imbued with some measure of those esteemed values.

40. Wai Keriba Ged

For the last time I stood briefly atop the aeolian peak of Erub... this ancient sentinel caressed by mystic zephyr...

The great eastern blue... blessing this domain through immemorial ages... rock, verdure, pacific oceanic winds and unknown essence... a unique and subtle scent pervading sweetness touching soul... the hint of something greater....

I did not want to leave.

The time spent in this ferociously peaceful realm had been far too short and yet... in some ways an eternity.

Part of me had always been here and forever will remain. Sadly I made my way down the hill..

And now....

My skiff would stay behind to guard my memories.

This small boat in the ocean had served me well these years through sun and storm adventures... It was to sit neglected in the mudflats of Port Douglas and in my absence, in time, would slowly rot back to the elements as if it had never been!

I was headed for Sydney...

*Occasionally these high intensity
highlights happened.
Every other day was extraordinary
in other ways!
There were many more adventures
but there's not enough room in
a small book such as this
to tell them all!*

Thumbnail of the Torres Strait Islands

There are an estimated 275 small islands in Torres Strait between Australia's Cape York Peninsula and Papua New Guinea. Of these, 17 Islands are inhabited.

They are:

TRADITIONAL NAME - ENGLISH NAME

Badu - Mulgrave Island
Boigu - Talbot Island
Dauan - Mt Cornwallis Island
Erub - Darnley Island
Keriri - Hammond Island
Mabuiag - Jervis Island
Masig - Yorke Island
Mer - Murray Island
Moa - Banks Island
Muralag - Prince of Wales Island
Ngarupai - Horn Island
Puruma - Coconut Island
Saibai - Saibai Island
Ugar - Stephen Island
Waiben - Thursday Island
Waraber - Sue Island
Yam -Turtle Backed Island

A multitude of species are now endangered because of extreme exploitation of the region. Some are already extinct.

Some populated islands are currently affected by rising water levels and are at risk.

Topography
The culturally unique Torres Strait Islander peoples' identity is connected to their ancestral homelands in the great shoal shelf known from time immemorial as 'Lumudhal.' To the west it was called 'Badu Hoki' and the region of deep waters at the eastern edge of the Great Barrier Reef was referred to as 'Koey.'

Within that great area of about 2,500 square kilometres, Islanders originally used the name of their home island to describe themselves. In the 1980's the term 'Zenadth Kes' came into being reclaiming the Lumudhal region to replace the appellation named after Luís Vaz de Torres, a Spanish maritime explorer of the 16th and 17th century. In the 1980's Adhi Ephraim Bani was inspired to create a descriptive amalgam of the geographical location of the island region based on the four winds to include the passageway between two continents thus: ZE – Zey (South) NA – Naygay (North) D – Dagam (Place/Side) TH – Thawathaw (Coastline) KES – Passage/Channel/ Waterway; developing the acronym 'Zenadth Kes.'

The Torres Strait Islands sprawl through the Zenadth Kes (Lumudhal region) which is the stretch of water that separates Cape York Peninsula in north Queensland from Papua New Guinea.

Astronomy, Ecology & Conservation
A rich heritage of practical astronomy forms a core aspect of Islander conservation lifestyle.

The stars provide seasonal references to survival and thriving. The hand of Tagai, the Southern Cross, points southward and enables navigation but more than that, various stellar configurations tell Islanders when conditions are most favourable to plant their food gardens, to hunt turtle and dugong, when the monsoon season is imminent, when the seasonal winds will change and informs daily life in many other ways.

Tagai indicates the cycles of nature and forecasts the wet season, the rising of Usal and Utimal in mid-November communicates turtle and dugong mating season and the time to plant gardens before the wet Kuki season. When Baidam constellation appears in the north the shark mating season starts and it's time to plant banana and cassava/manioc and other food staples.

Moon and tide phases tell the Islanders the best times to fish. Sun (girgir/gerger), moon (klsai)(each of numerous moon phases have a unique name) and stars (wer), land (apa), sea (ur) and sky (kotor) form vital branches of the Tree of Life, the life giving ecologies, without which no life on earth would be possible.

These are interwoven through spiritual beliefs, stories, songs and dances of the Torres Strait First Nations.

Seasons & Winds

There are four seasons associated with the wind changes in the Zenadth Kes environment - Kuki, Sager, Zey and Nay Gay.

KUKI (pronounced Cook-ee):
- North-West winds (strong winds)
- Blows from January until April
- Wet Season (monsoon)

SAGER (pronounced Sa-gerr):
- South-East trade winds
- Blows from May until December
- Dry season

ZEY (pronounced Zay):
- Southerly winds
- Blow randomly throughout the year

NAY GAY (pronounced Nai-gai):
- Northerly winds
- Blows from October until December
- Season when both heat and humidity are at their highest

Miriam Etymology of 'Lumudhal'
lu=thing, tree, ecosystem (implies growing out of foundation, source or root=giz foundation root)
mudal=place or house.

giz= point, seed, source, foundation, root
giz ged, n.=place of origin
le giz, an assemblage of le=people
Interestingly 'wer' can mean stars or sand.
Key stars have their own name in relation to the region. This is an intricate subject of study.

✳ A Tribute to Ion Llewellyn Idriess, [O.B.E.]

Ion (Jack) Idriess was one of my favourite authors.

He was writing before I was born and produced a huge number of classics such as Forty Fathoms Deep, Drums of Mer, The Cattle King, Gold Dust and Ashes, Coral Sea Calling, The Vanished People, Madman's Island, Headhunters of the Coral Sea, Nemarluk, The Diamonds, Across the Nullarbor and many more.

For some years when in the NSW Fire Brigades I was stationed at No 69 Dee Why Fire Station.

Unbeknownst to me he was living around the corner from the Fire Station.

How I would have loved to chat, share cups of tea and compare notes of our journeys after work.

But it was not to be as I had no way of knowing that he was there until in 1979 when I heard that he had died.

I was heartbroken to hear that such a great author had been so near and yet so far and that we could have met.

Like ships in the night we passed each other daily.

Salutations and respects Jack!

About the Author

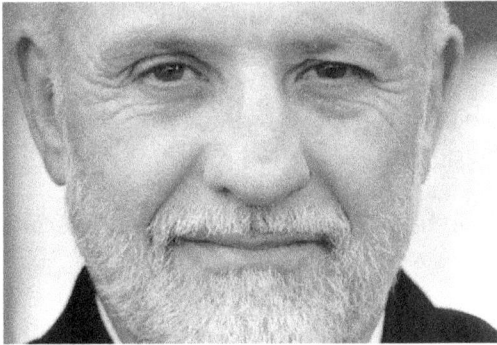

The author spent the early years of his life in Melbourne, Victoria. He then moved to Port Douglas in North Queensland in the 1960's and is the adopted son of a Torres Strait Island Elder. After spending time in the Torres Strait he moved to Sydney and after that, the Blue Mountains and beyond.

.

READ MORE
CLOSE SHAVES
& GEMS

Watch out for Book 2
New South Wales
CLOSE SHAVES
& GEMS

Book 1
Evan's
Torres Strait
CLOSE SHAVES & GEMS
ISBN: 978-0-9581444-0-7

ISBN 9780958144407

A catalogue record for this
book is available from the
National Library of Australia

NATIONAL
LIBRARY
OF AUSTRALIA

9 780958 144407

www.ingramcontent.com/pod-product-compliance
Lightning Source LLC
LaVergne TN
LVHW051548080426
835510LV00020B/2901